The Common Excuses of the Comfortable Compromiser

Understanding why people oppose your great idea

T0308684

The Common Excuses of the Comfortable Compromiser

Understanding why people oppose your great idea

Matt Crossman

BUSINESS BOOKS

Winchester, UK
Washington, USA

First published by Business Books, 2012
Business Books is an imprint of John Hunt Publishing Ltd., Laurel House, Station Approach,
Alresford, Hants, SO24 9JH, UK
office1@jhpbooks.net
www.johnhuntpublishing.com

For distributor details and how to order please visit the 'Ordering' section on our website.

Text copyright: Matt Crossman 2012

ISBN: 978 1 78099 595 3

A CIP catalogue record for this book is available from the British Library.

Design: Stuart Davies

Printed in the USA by Edwards Brothers Malloy

We operate a distinctive and ethical publishing philosophy in all
areas of our business, from our global network of authors to
production and worldwide distribution.

CONTENTS

Foreword

We live in the age of the compromiser. We know we need to change, but we can't because we fear we have too much to lose, so we compromise. This is a fundamental paradox facing human society. Comfortable compromisers often control the most significant power bases, meaning any attempt to argue for change in an area of personal or public life is met with a barrage of familiar excuses. Since the current situation serves them well, they have little interest or incentive to listen to arguments for change. They can see both sides of the argument, but since the assignment of benefits is currently stacked in their favour, they don't wish to meddle. Political, business and personal life all echo with the sound of compromise.

Having identified our subject of study, we can observe their traits and habits. Through careful observation we observe nine distinct and identifiable calls of the compromiser, their common excuses and objections which are always at hand. The common excuses and resistance to change flow from common human frailties, or the tendency to place too much weight on the importance of certain ideas. In our filed guide to the common excuses of the compromiser we deal with the excuses in three rough categories. First, we explore those psychological and behavioural traits which lead us down blind alleys, and to repeating our mistakes. Then we look at our over-reliance on certain concepts and ideas which similarly give the illusion of sense while blinding us to other possibilities. Finally, we explore more societal issues, including our feeling of personal responsibility, and the notion of timing of decisions.

Throughout, we reflect on the ways in which these weaknesses and fears are played upon, amplified and used by the compromisers who seek to avoid the change society as a whole needs. We extrapolate personal observations into insights into our 'corporate life' - a term I shall use to mean the arena in which human beings interact as groups with distinct and overlapping groups. This includes the political sphere and policy debate, but also the many other areas of life in which we find ourselves playing advocate or defendant, victim or perpetrator. I refer to work life, community life in leisure or philanthropic institutions, but also domestic life. In each chapter we explore the common excuse in some detail, seeking to understand just what it is that makes us behave the way we do, such that we can be exploited in arguments and debates.

We face great floods of negativity from those pre-disposed by their material or social position to oppose things and make excuses for difficult situations. It is this negative state of mind which we seek to understand and deal with. The obstacles can seem insurmountable; but many an objection has an appearance of menace masking a conformity to currently ideology, defeatable once recognised. This book serves as a general 'primer' for anyone involved in the process of campaigning or driving change, but should also be read by anyone puzzled or confused at their own lack of consistency, and failure to deliver the changes in your own sphere of influence that you know are needed. You will find yourself identifying with both compromiser and advocate for change, and gain a fresh insight into the need for innovative and pristine ideas on which to base our interactions as a society.

Inspiration

"We have to gird ourselves against the unholy trinity of reactionary rhetoric identified by the great development economist Albert Hirschman. He noted that every new idea for constructive change is met with three attacks. The first is futility; the course of reform cannot work because the problem is insolvable. The second is perversity; any attempt at solving the problem will make matters worse. The third is jeopardy; attempting to solve the problem will take attention and resources away from something even more important. *This negativism is a state of mind, not a view based on facts. Vigorous debate over the methods of change is, of course, healthy and vital, but relentless acceptance of the status quo is not acceptable in the face of the challenges we confront.*" Jeffery Sachs

Thanks

To Anne, for your love, beauty and encouragement.

Tom, Liz, Olly, Joel and Mr. Pillowhead for keeping me grounded and semi-sane while writing my first book.

Perry and John at Rathbones for their encouragement and granting of my sabbatical.

Mum and Dad for their constant support, love, helpful criticism and comments.

Ben for listening to my ideas as we run in the woods, refining blue sky thinking through the mind of an entrepreneur.

ADH and the rest of the Bristol community for conversations, coffee and WB.

The Vancouver Public Library System for giving me desk space, and the University of Bristol for allowing their graduates free access to their library facilities.

About the Author

Matt Crossman has a legal background, and has worked for the last seven years in the responsible investment field, engaging with major global companies at a senior management level. He has served on the board of an NGO engaging with global companies on issues of human rights, environmental protection and corporate responsibility for the last four years. In addition, he is a trustee for LoveBristol (Release 2010, "Unputdownable" – the Bristol Festival of Literature), an innovative urban development charity which has ambitious plans for seeing community-led, holistic and creative urban redevelopment.

Matt's short but intensive experience in public debates over ethical issues combined with efforts to encourage policy makers, companies and government departments towards creative solutions to difficult problems gives him an excellent perspective on the common tactics used to defend the status quo.

Drawing from his wide ranging experience, reading across a number of fields of study and areas of expertise, he presents easily digestible but thought provoking issue summaries and tactical guides, helping the reader feel better equipped to enter into discourse on the trickiest issues.

Chapter 1

But It Could Be Worse

Our first excuse should be familiar to anyone who's ever tried to change anything. Whatever the shortcomings of the current situation, the compromiser sees that things could always be worse. Much of modern politics relies on this uneasy accord, preferring to deal with the known shortcomings of the familiar rather than risk opening up to a whole suite of scary, unfamiliar issues. Rarely will an issue be black and white, a choice between unadulterated wickedness and purest virtue. Instead, an issue will be presented in a kaleidoscope of shades of grey, in which the current situation rests easy because there are darker, blacker options seemingly equally as likely. A fundamental bias exists here, since we will always know more about what we have been doing for years than is possible for us to know about suggested actions that have yet to be taken. The change agent therefore needs to carefully consider how best to make his case, bearing in mind this fundamental 'inequality of information' that exists between the past and the future, and our preference for dealing with problems that are familiar to us.

A necessary 'Evil'

In an effort to refine our views on world issues, my colleagues and I once embarked on a noble project; the wall of good and evil. Taking our cue from the popular BBC TV Show Top Gear and their 'cool wall' (in which new cars are presented to the crowd by the team, who then debate whether the car is cool or not; cue banter), we endeavoured to rank technologies, people and companies on a sliding scale of good and evil. I would reproduce a photograph of the wall in its latest incarnation, but the former law student in me fears being sued for character assassination at best, and treason at worst.

The fun came in calibrating the wall. We couldn't just place the companies and technologies randomly on the wall - we needed to know what counted as 'very' good and 'very' evil. So we embarked on a process of calibration - nominating great figures from history and current political figureheads, and gradually we arrived at a useable scale.[1] Every week on Friday once the day's work was done, and before weekend drinks, people could nominate additions to the wall of good and evil.

It was a fantastic source of office comedy and bonding on one hand - but on another was a pretty serious indicator of the diversity of opinions even within a semi-social enterprise. After a few months the wall became full on nominees, but was also the subject of vandalism. People who disagreed with the location of certain historical figures would, in dead of night, unilaterally move their political hero or villain left or right. If memory serves, Margaret Thatcher was the most moved figure on the wall. Oil companies and arms companies were the second most moved and the most debated. The most common argument? "We *need* x, y or z".

I proposed adding another axis - that of necessity. It may be evil - it may be dirty, and unappetising, but this can be excused because 'we' need it. A case in point is the mining industry. A difficult activity to manage and regulate, with a full suite of accompanying social and environmental issues. However, modern life - be it your house, your car, or even the laptop I write on - depends on the extraction of energy sources, metals or rare earth elements for electronics.

The 'necessity' question comes down to weighing up the benefits against the costs. For example, the social contract surrounding medical animal testing rests on necessity; we need medicine to protect human life, therefore it is excusable to test the potentially beneficial drugs on animals who may be harmed in the process. This is a simplification of a very complex debate, but it makes the point - sometimes the end justifies the means.

But can you sacrifice everything at the altar of necessity? Isn't everything capable of being described as vital, depending on what different people would regard as being impossible to do without? There are some things most of us could agree on as being vital - the use of animals to test vaccines which save the lives of thousands, for example - but what of mining mentioned above? We may enjoy our smart-phones and our laptops, but is it necessary to our health and wellbeing; in fact, could it be argued that overuse of technology is detrimental to our health?

Assessing Risk

This excuse is interesting because it does not seek to defend the status quo on the basis of its inherent benefits. Nobody is suggesting that the way we do things now is "the best"; instead, it is the "least worst" of all the options available to us. The current abortion rules in the UK could be seen in this light. It is a very difficult and highly emotive subject, with many convincing arguments on all sides. Balancing protection of the mother versus that of the unborn child, the law makes several distinctions which are difficult for many to grasp. But however queasy one might feel, the reality is that the weakest and the most vulnerable were being harmed by back-street abortion. Things have undoubtedly moved further towards 'lifestyle' choice abortion in recent years, but the core trade off remains the same. Harm was being done while this activity was illegal, hence we had to do something. Sometimes, a risky course of action will be preferred because the risks, though real, are known quantities.

Nearly all human activities involve some trade off between risk and benefit. The situations we face are uncertain, and the options we have available to us are numerous, one of which is usually more undesirable than the others. We judge some risks to be acceptable due to the benefits we derive, such as driving a car despite the risk of an accident. The easiest cases to object to, and hence to argue against their change, are those where risks are run with no discernible benefit to anyone. But these cases are very rare, and most of us must deal with the balancing of different risks and rewards on a daily basis.

Assessing risk is something we all do every day, even something basic as assessing the risk of being caught. I live in a large shared house with 20 other people. We should all replace the milk from the stores when it runs out. This involves a short walk to the basement, and a minute's inconvenience. If there are others in the kitchen, we will change the milk, because we run the risk of being called on our behaviour if someone else is there. If no-one's there, there is no enforcement likely and so we run the risk of making the selfish choice. Countless choices present themselves every hour. Every time we use medication we are submitting to the risk of side-effects identified in the packaging we never read. Every time we drive a car we are submitting to the risk of an accident for the sake of the benefits of private transportation.

Risk assessment for the big issues facing society is more problematic than these more common situations, since people do not really understand the problems with assessing risk in a meaningful way. Let's consider how we can assess risk, and the various factors we must look at. Firstly, consequences; some are reversible, others are not. Generally, people think it more appropriate to run the risk of a relatively reversible harm than an irreversible one. This links with a second factor, that of the severity of the impact. Running a small risk of a small harm may be acceptable; running a small risk of a devastating catastrophe may not. Or we may just not know how harmful something is, while we may know exactly what risk we run of encountering it. Finally, the full effects of some risked impacts will be felt at different timescales. We may feel very differently about the probability of a medium sized harm occurring once in a year, against once in a lifetime.

Most uneasy compromises will be justified in some way consistent with this analysis. Usually supported by dodgy stats, or at least very generously interpreted trends and data, they will present the risks as manageable, defined and clearly worth risking for the private and public benefit.

Sadly, for something we do every day, we are pretty poor assessors of risk. Studies show that we rarely hit the nail on the head, and tend to under or over estimate risk compared with the observable statistical relationship[2]. At a basic level, we consider those everyday, familiar hazards to be much less risky than they actually are. But there is more going on here than a cold calculation of my risk of injury from a particular product or activity; it is much more idiosyncratic. Our feelings about something will inform our value judgement about the likelihood of a risk, and our perception of its severity. Our past experiences will affect our feelings, as will our level of information and capacity to understand that information. Those risks which we generally consider to be faced voluntarily are usually judged as less serious than those which are imposed upon us.

Those risks with which we are familiar appear to us to be better managed, better controlled and more worth running. This helps us understand the power of this excuse even further. Its effect is even more powerful when the "Evil" we prefer is something we have chosen, something which we voluntarily expose ourselves to, compared with any number of potential more serious consequences which may be imposed on us from the outside.

But how much harm is allowable in pursuit of the good? If we return to animal testing, we might easily justify the saving of a few hundred thousand children's lives for the sake of 2,000 mice. If the numbers are changed, we may see problems, leading our argument down a cul-de-sac. If we were to kill exactly the same number of mice per human saved, what then? What if the ratio was 2:1?

If someone asks you where you draw the line, do not cave in immediately. If your opposer has evidence to support his premise, listen. Perhaps the questioner has evidence that the number of mice being used is increasing, or procedures are becoming more harmful, meaning that the balance of harm and benefits needs to be reassessed. The point is that issues of scale can *always* be drawn out, for every issue. Rarely are the issues that generic; they are usually specific. With the mice, we are not talking about a procedure which would kill animals and save humans on a 1:1 basis, but a much better ratio. The specific context is important.

The disjunction tactic

The manifestation of this excuse has a defining characteristic - that of contrast. The problems of the present can be made to feel less serious when contrasted with an imagined future which is unspeakably awful. Things are a mixture of good and bad, but could be worse, so it's best to stick with what we've got. Any compromise looks more attractive when compared to a fictional doomsday scenario. Rather than addressing the actual debate on an established practice, a comparison is made to the worst case, however fanciful and unrealistic it may be. Reducing a debate to two options, one of which is manifestly a terrible option is characterised by those who study such things as 'binaries' or 'disjunctions'.

Social scientists suggest that these 'binaries' or dichotomies constitute a good deal of public discourse. Going beyond the simple use of disjunctions, such binary representations of issues come loaded with a number of assumptions. Consider such debates as nature/nurture, legalise/criminalise, uncivilised/ civilised; these depictions assume an exclusion - an either / or. What is on one side a debate cannot be on another, and if you try and argue from a more nuanced point of view, you are vulnerable to attack.

Understanding this aspect of our compromisers' first general excuse is aided by analysis of argument which has been conducted by academics such as Richard Feldman. Direct comparisons are described by Feldman as simple "or" statements. The argument is one of elimination - "it's either this or that, and no-one in their right mind believes THAT will work, so it must be this".

The argument is valid, in its own terms, since it makes superficial sense. It is the premise that is false - the idea that there are only two options available to us. According to Feldman:

> "...There are many realistic arguments that do follow this pattern ... one context in which this occurs is reasoning about social policies, as when someone says "Either you support the BX missile or you are for a strong defense (sic). There may well be another alternative; you are for a strong defense, but you think there are better ways to achieve (it) than through the BX missile."[3]

The pattern is to compare your preferred option with some 'ridiculous premise which can easily be disproved' - 'the argument seems to establish the preferred alternative by ruling out the ridiculous option'[4]. We might say the preferred alternative is 'excused' by the mythical option to which it is compared.

Of course, in the real world you will likely not encounter this form of argument in quite as clear a light as presented here. It may be hidden in paragraph after paragraph of data and opinion, but it might still boil down to the simple argument with a flawed premise; its either X, or Y, and the alternative is so unthinkably awful that we must do X. This appeals to most of us who long for simplicity and brevity, but masks deeper and more complicated issues.

The Sound of the Underground

The common argument that 'Things that could be worse' in fact consists of many common sub-arguments, specific and general ways in which most things could be worse. Especially in the realm of social policy, where we seek to regulate behaviours which entail a mixture of harm and benefits, there is usually some debate over the legality of a behaviour. More often than not it will argued that a controversial activity is better legalised and out in the open than criminalised and forced underground.

Exploring the American experiment with prohibition of alcohol reveals many of the problems associate with driving an activity underground, and illustrates the effect of another ghost which haunts the change-agent - unintended consequences. Prior to prohibition, social drinking in a gathered context had generally been something enjoyed by men. In the Prohibition era, women came to the party. Many of our now classic cocktail recipes hark back to the days when the operators of speakeasies concocted new ways of masking the often unpalatable moonshine for the female palate. But there were more serious consequences of driving the industry underground, consequences which the well-meaning reformers failed to predict.

Making alcohol is not straightforward, as any young man who has endured a disaster with a home-brew kit will inform you.[5] Basic brewing is relatively easy, but still carries risks. Further distilling this alcohol involves high temperatures and pressures. Modern brewing and distilling operations are complex industrial processes, tightly regulated and constrained by health legislation. Moonshiners are subject to no such scrutiny, nor are they traceable once poor product is discovered. Injured people have no legal cause to pursue against those who have caused them harm.

In cases such as this, the activity is illegal, and yet being pursued underground, providing unscrupulous individuals with the opportunity to exploit others. When debating such issues there can be very compelling arguments on both sides of the debate. The choice of policy makers in such cases in unenviable. Passionate people with good arguments on both sides will vie for your attention, but in the mean time innocent people are being hurt. Better to choose one, compromise now to avoid further harm. - or so the excuse goes.

Brinksmanship

How might this excuse show itself in business life? In negotiation theory, this use of the disjunction as an excuse would be classified as brinksmanship. As a last resort, a negotiator may reduce the argument down to a 'binary', a disjunction, in order to force someone's hand. An opposition party will try and push you to the brink, in order to extract greater concessions from you. Fans of 1950's American youth culture might also recognise a link with playing 'chicken'; two drivers hurtle towards a ravine, the first one to pull up loses his car. It's a gamble, with a big downside, a question of who blinks first. As a tactic, its strength is also its weakness, since it turns negotiation into a serious game in which one or both of the parties find it difficult to distinguish reality from postured negotiation positions.

Brinksmanship has parallels with what is termed "playing hardball" - that is, making aggressive and pressuring moves in order to short-circuit debate to get what you want, pushing people into agreements they would rather not make. Hardball tactics take two main forms, firstly showing your own position in a more favourable light, or secondly making your other options seem less suitable. Either way, we observe once again the pattern of reductionism, taking the complex and making it appear simple.

Our fear of everything

Stating "it could be worse" can have an effect which is subtly different from the binary / disjunction argument tactic above, but one which still rests on forcing people to make decisions based on false choices. Instead, it can seek to manipulate our fears for the future, introducing not one but *numerous* horrific alternatives, adding complexity and an overwhelming negativity which may force people into abiding by the status quo. Basing your future strategy on your numerous fears about what might be round the corner is an easy trap to fall into. We all do some basic theorising about what risks may befall us, and we seek to minimise their potential impact. But what's true and sensible at a personal level can be inefficient and dumb at a more corporate level. In decision making at the personal level, we can arrive at a set of value judgements of the alternatives before us, based on our values and our subjective assessment of the likelihood and desirability of the options before us. Doing this in a group involves adding up all of these subjective preferences into one entity - a difficult task. In fact, it's so difficult as to be impossible. There is no way you will be able to include every variable into your model for making a decision. Such rational choices, for groups, are inherently incomplete. This leaves rooms for creative suggestions of fears.

Especially in the realm of public security, people can take a doomsday approach to risk management which can lead to inefficient systems which are nonetheless defended and entrenched. Policy is too often based on "what if?" scenarios, fictional conceptions of dangers which might befall you. The problem is that these scenarios develop not from scientific enquiry and careful observation, but fear and imagination. Hence they are limitless, and each one needs only to be thought of as plausible, not probable, to get acted upon.

Airline security is one such area best with this problem. With the horrific security failures of 9/11 still fresh in the memory, policy is being made in an ad hoc and sporadic manner, as the regulators are desperate to prevent any implication in any further security failings. Despite the fact they are a known group, subject to more prescribed and effective constraints on their behaviour, airline staff undergo the same security checks as passengers. You might be able to demonstrate that such a group are a much lower risk, but the answer comes back - "what if?" What if a pilot's brother was killed in Afghanistan and the pilot, filled with rage against established Christianity, converted to Islam, was radicalised, became an Al Qaeda operative and crashed the 0900 from JFK into the statue of Liberty? No-one's denying that it *could* happen - and with the wounds of 9/11 still raw, there is no real argument with someone in this situation. But the more sensible question is whether it is statistically *likely* to happen, and whether effective controls exist to stop it happening among the limited number of people who would have access to the opportunity repeat the act.

Exploring a real world compromise

We've seen how debates are reduced into black and whites, and how the compromisers manipulate our fear of the future to force into false choices in theory, and given some isolated examples. Now we need to consider how this excuse behaves in a real-world compromise.

Those profiting from apparel industry love to tell you how things 'could be worse'. In the old Western economies, globalisation has benefitted our wardrobes with cheap fashion. However, of late there has been a great awakening in awareness of the poor conditions suffered by those at the dirty, back street, sweatshop end of clothing manufacture. Since the compromisers - those making money out of the situation, and those benefitting from the cheap clothing - have been presented with the negative aspects of the trade in recent years, there has been a corresponding growth in the use of disjunctions in the discourse surrounding the industry.

High-profile companies have faced campaigns from Non Governmental Organisations (NGOs) exposing poor working conditions, low wages and denial of basic human rights. The companies respond in various ways to these accusations. If they do not take the route of denial (either denying a problem entirely, or recognising a problem with the entire industry, while maintaining that they are whiter than white), then the route of pragmatism is the most popular. They may admit that things look bad on the surface, but assert the relative benefits of the existence of their trading relationship compared with no industry at all. Low wages are an issue - but unemployment is a bigger one. In essence, the disjunction is also brinksmanship in action. Who will blink first - the employee who faces termination from his role if he continues to complain, or the company who threatens to withdraw all investment in an area if they are pursued too vigorously?

All of this makes an easy compromise for the company. They recognise to some degree that there is a problem - but a follow it up with a collective shrug of the shoulders, somehow suggesting that the meagre benefits derived from the the current situation be appreciated by those at the bottom of the pile. How convenient. Those exploited should be grateful, and the company can rest easy, having removed any compulsion to raise standards.

Raising the spectre of a withdrawal of investment is closely related to another element of the excuse that 'things could be worse'. In this case, it is not just the absence of activity that is scary, but the risk of who might step into the gap should the company in question withdraw. Classically, this has been used by companies operating in weak-governance zones, or those with lower standards of regulation. A company from a relatively well-regulated home state, with strong policies on employment rights, environmental management and stakeholder relations is criticised for conducting a controversial project in a geopolitical context where enforcement of such rules, if they exist at all, is weak. NGOs and concerned stakeholders complain that the project tarnishes the company's otherwise sound reputation.

The company's response goes something like this;

> "We hear you. We know there are problems on the ground in country X. We have difficulty recruiting the right people, and retaining them, and further difficulty overseeing them. We, just like you, want the highest standards to be met in our operations, since we a good citizen. However, there are forces outside of our control, and we have to manage with what we can achieve. If conditions cannot be improved, then you insist that we pull out. But that will create a void to be filled by a much less scrupulous operator. We're listening and talking, and doing a best. But if we pull out, the companies that will take our place won't give a damn, and wont even answer the phone to you. So what do you want to do? Criticise us so we pull out, and deal with the "devil"? Or do you want to work with us to solve the problem?"

On a superficial level this has validity - but only if the threat is real. If it is imaginary, then you can attack at for what it is, a disguise for compromise. Most projects like this are profitable, otherwise the company wouldn't be risking the approbation of society is pursuing their goals. How likely is it that such a company would up sticks, abandon its investment in infra-structure and relationships with powerful institutions and leave a competitor to benefit?

Dealing with the "Devil"

Confronting the argument is best achieved by pointing out the reductionist duality on which your opponent is resting his case (Although going round accusing people of being reductionist dualists is unlikely to add many folk to your Christmas card list). Reducing a complicated issued down to a black and white choice is immature, shallow and unhelpful. Pointing this out in careful language makes you look like the adult, and the more reasoned partner. You can sympathise with your opponent in a slightly condescending way - "well, I wish it really were that simple, then we could all live in happiness". The other option is rather obvious, and that is to mention the other options that exist. But that is time consuming, and the more elements you introduce into your argument, the harder it is to understand, which is precisely why the simple disjunction wins so much superficial support.

The social scientists Lewicki, Saunders and Barry offer some options for dealing with such excuses when they are used as negotiation tactics. Firstly, you can just ignore them. In public debate, not responding to a threat can be a powerful way of defusing the situation. The other party is feeling challenged , and hence has moved on to hardball tactics, in which case you can feel more confident in your underlying case. Stay calm, and try and change the subject. Better still, reduce the adversarial feeling by getting other parties involved in the debate.

A second way of dealing with hardball is to discuss them - "that is, label the tactic and indicate to the other party that you know what he/she is doing"[6] This is less about discussing the specifics of the Faustian choice offered you, as much as it is recognising that the tactic is being used against you. Shift the discussion to focus on the very method of discussion to be used. You may recognise the other person is being 'hard', and politely remind them that you can be 'hard' as well. But you would much rather move away from such adversarial confrontations and seek better, more productive ways forward for both parties. This is similar to the negotiating technique of 'flagging up' points of contention.

Thirdly, should these polite reminders fall on deaf, compromised ears, you can fight fire with fire, and escalate the situation with your own hardball tactics. This may earn you the respect of some 'strong' opponents, who may have simply begun with hardball tactics because they suspect you are weak and are testing your resolve. However, this is a risky strategy, as it can result in chaos, produce hard feelings, and be counter-productive, according to Lewicki et al.

There are countless more such techniques catalogued in social science volumes. Learning from these situations gives us some really useful insights into how to deal with the "Devil". In short, the 'binary' is not serious comment on the issues, but a means to an end, a powerful tactic which is designed to win short term support. It can be met with similar negotiation tactics, as above. If you've successfully defused the disjunction, what then? Now you can attempt to shape the debate by introducing more reasoned argument.

Controlling the issues

Arguments and debates can escalate when the parties throw all kinds of extraneous issues into the ring. Typically, as conflicts intensify, the size, number and complexity of the issues being discussed expands.[7] The larger the conflict, the harder it will be to resolve. This is why using the 'fear of everything that could be worse' is an effective tool, since it adds layer upon layer of complexity on already difficult issues, exacerbating our human tendency towards despondency when faced with hardship or trial as we've noted above.

The skilled negotiator will therefore have a number of techniques for controlling the extent of the discussion, keeping 'issue proliferation' under control. In public discourse this is problematic, since anyone who has an opinion can voice it through whichever media they have available to them. In private discourse, the core technique involves 'fractioning'[8]. This involves splitting and separating out the issues and the parties. For example, you may agree before hand exactly who you will meet with, and keep the number of extra parties to a minimum, or agree what the substantive issues, and agree their definition.

In dialogue with companies, reducing the number of parties is an oft-repeated battle. Frequently, the company will try and out-number you. If you haven't been sidelined already by a representative from the corporate communications or community relations teams, then you will be introduced at the last minute to members from the legal, finance or compliance teams, or a consultant. The wider the discussion, the less likely a useful substantive outcome. Agreeing the parties beforehand can keep things manageable, or at least prepare you for a wider discussion.

Offering hope

If we've come this far, and managed to make the opponent see the downside of the current uneasy compromise, we will need to suggest better interventions than the choices being presented to us. This can be a major stumbling block in any debate, if we are not prepared for it. We need to dedicate research onto closing the gap between the vast amount of information we have on the way we currently do things and the relative lack of information on the effects of what we might do differently. On the spectrum of possible interventions between legalisation and prohibition, calls for repeal of restrictions often face one large and important mountain to climb. Yes, we know the current system has flaws; but what else can we do?

If you're pushing for repeal, it is important to have a viable alternative[9] lined up so you can't be easily sidelined as someone shouting from the edges of a debate with no solutions. However, it is not vital to have solved the problem. Last week my lawn mower had hit a rock and bent the blade, meaning it was more rotary cultivator than lawn mower. My gardening colleague didn't know the first thing about motorised lawn mowers and how to fix them, but he was dead right to shout at me and tell me to stop. A criticism of an existing problem is still valid even if you don't know exactly how to fix it!

At risk of sounding evangelical, the "Devil" excuse rests on the effect of fear, so the best way to deal with it is to use hope. Not an abstract flimsy optimism but an unshakeable belief in the ability of human society to gradually improve, and learn from its mistakes. Not fluffy, nebulous claims, but real examples of how things have changed and been done differently, of men and women who put their hope to work. Unless you're at complete rock bottom, all manner of things in your life could be worse, given enough bad luck. This also creates the possibility that whatever benefits you are currently receiving, things could also be better. There are very few situations in which the general compromise which society has reached are representative of a genuine failure to find any better way of doing things. Abortion seems to be one such instance, but is a peculiarly difficult and intricate issue. In the vast majority of situations and arguments you face, when someone claims that things could be worse, it is most likely to be a hardball tactic, a disjunction intended to force other's hands. In these situations, once you recognise the use of the tactic you can move the debate on. Life is more complicated and more interesting than the simple choices beloved of PR firms who delight in presenting everything as a black and white choice. Your skill will be introducing different hues into the debate in a way which empowers rather than alienates those involved. But what if these flashy, hopeful suggestions have been tried before?

Chapter 2

But We've Tried Before - And Failed

I'm assuming you've all been there, in the meeting room, when the new person suggests we try to fix the problem we're facing by doing this or that. You smirk, and make a knowing glance to the other established members of the team as you remember the precious hours of your life that you wasted trying to do just that, and failing spectacularly. Or perhaps you've been on the therapist's couch discussing issues of your early childhood, and the time you ran in the egg and spoon race, only to trip, fall, and expose yourself to the ridicule of the gathered parents and peers. At that moment, shrouded in failure, you swore never to repeat your mistake and have not taken part in any competitive sport since. The memory of failure runs deep in us, especially since our society places so much value on visible and material success. We excuse our current inaction with reference to our own internal chronicle of broken promises and failed efforts. It is possible to excuse any inaction or compromise by raising even the suggestion of past failures.

Our life in organisations is similarly afflicted by the effect of failures. Appreciating the feelings and motivations of the members of an organisation which moved from apathy to action only to fail is vital to engaging with this excuse for inaction. Not just our own failures, but those of others frequently enter into the debate. In fact, fear of failure is often used in conjunction with our first excuse, that things could be worse. Other people's failures are used to create pressure for reluctant acceptance of the problematic but familiar status quo.

As we watch human life develop and grow, we see that experimentation, failure and refinement of ideas are fundamental. On a personal level, our attempts to try new things can result in success or failure, pain or pleasure. Fear of failure can often result in us never even starting a project. For the most part we accept the trade-off, enjoying our success and knowing that failures better prepare us for future successes. However, the fear of failure and the long-lasting effects of previous disasters of our own making can lead both individuals and organisations into a defensive position, fearing anything new in case it raises the spectre of failure once again. How do we begin to engage with an organisation who's most powerful argument against your proposal is that the exact same tactics or ideas have been tried before and have failed?

Misdiagnosis and Apathy

Collective apathy is crippling; but frequently people are less apathetic towards a specific change than they are pessimistic that they can make any sort of meaningful contribution. Human beings are creatures dependent on good rhythms of rest, food and encouragement. Even the best of us can get weighed down by the cares of the world, laden by worries and worn down by refusals and failures. Often a group can become too aware of its limitations, and whilst its values would lead it to agree with you or assist in your work, past experience stops them.

Feeling like we've tried before and failed, having used the same techniques and changes which were supposed to help but didn't, can grow out of a basic but important error; misdiagnosis of the underlying problem. If we do not see the problem as a whole, but rather try to deal with the multiple 'symptoms' it causes, then we will fail to deal with the root of the issue.

Think of the workers at a computer technology processing company who when surveyed seemed to be concerned about a great deal of aspects of their work life - and articulated their problems as the 'lack' of certain benefits - the ability to chat with coworkers as in other office jobs, free drinks, flexible hours and the like. Little was said about the experience itself at first. They intuitively knew something was wrong with the job, but couldn't articulate it.

After working with a consultant, they identified a loss of sense of self, feeling liking a robot, boredom and alienation as the key problems. The researcher in question suggested that action to ameliorate matters needed to be directed at the work situation itself, and not - or not only - at the fringe benefits. Imagine that this reflection had not been forthcoming, and flexitime had been introduced, or free coffee for all staff at 11am. The benefits are marginal, and crucially, the staff realise this, and so experience a proportionately greater disappointment. The workers embarked on a subconscious 'fragmentation' of the core problem, and then projected these fragmented aspects onto the atmosphere of the job.

If we're aware of our own short-sightedness and know that we need some external perspective, we must also be cautious about how we gain those third-party insights. Companies and organi-sations do many things and invest significant resources in order to get different perspectives - setting up focus groups, bringing in consultants, buying in different expertise or acquiring companies from a different part of the market. The danger is that these views will be presented in too favourable light - for example, a consultant is much less likely get more work from the company if they let loose a visceral attack on their paymasters!

Our misdiagnosis of the problem can also lead to a blind belief that actions which have proven to fail once before will really work this time. This is because the problem has not been diagnosed, only the symptoms. There is considerable overlap here with 'path dependency', a concept we will look at more in a forthcoming chapter. There is then a need to diagnose the whole problem and lead the group or organisation into an awareness of the true nature of its condition. Only then can the group effec-tively 'learn' as an institution, and break free from the cycle of failure, apathy and misplaced faith in inadequate solutions.

Worse than trying, failing and retreating is identifying the problems with our past strategy and then not implementing a new system for dealing with them. I have recent personal experience of this weakness having recently installed a new fireplace in my shared house. My workmate and I were going to fix the skirting boards back on, paint them and finish the job. Except, we couldn't find the things. Whoever had taken them off had placed them next to the fire, but they weren't there.

You can probably guess what had happened. They got burnt as kindling. Disaster. So we found some old timber, and measured the pieces up to re-fit them once the plaster dried. I left at this point, but when I came back, the skirting boards were once again stacked very close to the wood pile, and it's easy to see how the mistake could very easily be repeated, leading to a significant increased failure rate in our renovation efforts. We had numerous options available to us, including warning signs, leaving notes, group emails, locking up the fire lighters, etc, all of which were suggested. But the most simple and elegant was what we should have done in the first place - moved the timber to a place where it could not be mistaken for firewood. Having recognised our error, we needed to adjust our systems to avoid its repetition. This often easier said than done!

Moving on from banal personal observations, let's involve a real academic heavyweight. Stephen M Walt is a professor in International affairs at Harvard University, and has written extensively on the lack of understanding of failure in foreign policy. Of several telling examples, none was more serious for mankind than the experience of the rise of the Nazi party in the early part of the of twenty first century. A generation of Germans had experienced at first hand the devastating downside of of a failed quest for political dominance of Europe; yet twenty years later, they were led down the same path. How did a society forget the costs of the past, one paid in the lives of its young men? Clearly 'learning the right lessons and remembering them over time, is a lot harder than it seems'.[10]

Part of this is down to the relative lack of feedback. As we have already discussed, getting adequate understanding of the past is vital in safeguarding your future from the same errors. This is true for all areas of life, but is much easier to apply in technical fields such as engineering, where the chain of causality is more easily established. This is not to say that engineers never make mistakes, as the history of failed building projects with design flaws would undermine that contention at a stroke, but it is to say that looking back at historical events, ones which depend on human agency, emotion and conflicting motive, must necessarily provide weaker feedback. In criminology, or social policy, it is often much harder to say for certain whether a particular intervention genuinely helped improve a situation; it's therefore easier for a failing policy to continue to be used.

When situations change, prompting dire need for re-evaluation, its important to point of that the mere existence of new technology doesn't mean that every previously discredited policy or approach will suddenly become successful. Walt again provides an excellent example, this time mentioning the over-confidence of the financial industry in rolling out new models of risk analysis which would 'overcome the laws of economic gravity ... permitting a vast expansion of new credit with little risk of financial collapse'. Don't worry about past debt bubbles bursting, things are different now, we've got the computers. Except they weren't, and we're still feeling the pain.

If you're convinced that something's a bad idea, then logically speaking, why is it even there to oppose? Why do bad ideas persist? Usually because someone somewhere is getting a benefit from the compromise. Debate and dialogue should ensure the 'right' policies emerge, but 'Self-interested actors who are deeply committed to a particular agenda can distort the marketplace of ideas'.[11] Challenging the continued existence of an obviously 'bad idea' is less about debating the issues as navigating the social context. The slavery debate illustrates this perfectly. The humanity of the situation and attitude to human cruelty shifted, but a privileged class of traders who had made their fortunes stood in the way of abolition. It is not spoken of much, but these traders were financially compensated, creating the space for abolition to proceed. A warning from recent history comes in the US market for corn-based ethanol. Subsidised as a potential low-carbon fuel (now widely discredited as a clean energy source) farmers who converted their lands to corn crops are heavily reliant on the continued subsidy. Unfortunately, the same farmers are disproportionately represented in the states which decide early on the nominations for the US presidential race. To oppose an obviously inefficient and failed green strategy would be political suicide, so the subsidy continues.[12]

Empathy between generations is running at a low ebb in British society, which also creates the atmosphere for repeating failures. Our current culture is dominated by youth - everything young is 'cool', and so we don't really respect the lessons of the past as we should. We shut ourselves off from the feedback of past generations.[13] Some feel that we have entered into such a time of disruptive, rapid change that there are fewer benefits from the insight of past generations. Against this I can only offer anecdotal evidence from my family. My Grandpa worked for 40 years in the same company, rising from a very junior position to being an international executive. My Father had several different careers, from research, to teaching, to management in the charity sector and consultancy. On the face of it, my Grandpa's experi-ences of a career seem less helpful - which of us stays 4 years in the same job let alone 40 years? He used to manage the estab-lishment of temporary land-line communications in rural England so that harvests could be better timed, the kind of mass logistical exercise which is now achieved by one farmer and an internet connection. But the truth is that my Grandpa is a wealth of wisdom and understanding, for one massively important reason; he dealt with people. His experience of managing personnel, petty conflicts, pay rises and job cuts stand the test of time. I still benefit from the wisdom he gained from his failures. However 'disruptive' technological changes may become, we are still a civilisation of relational creatures, and so there will always be value to the 'feedback' we receive from past generations, run through our current cultural filters of course.

Pessimism?

Those using the examples of past failure to excuse current inaction can be pigeon holed as merely pessimists, those with a general negative attitude. Is life really divided into optimists and pessimists? I would imagine you could immediately suggest a few people in your life who would fit into either category. There's usually one very prominent pessimist in your immediate social context. They are typically well aware of risks, and are therefore usually risk-averse. They are usually highly cautious, aware of dangers (real or perceived), and well acquainted with the scare stories told by others.

Having encountered pessimism in the form of this argument, is there any hope for the situation? Answering this question depends if you believe that pessimism and optimism are in-built into a person's psyche or are learned behaviours. The answer is fascinating in itself - optimists believe their optimism is learnt. Pessimists *know* that it isn't. Frequently we learn that pessimism is in fact linked to the subject's general state of happiness. Recent failure lives long in the mind, creating a depressive cloud hanging over everything you do. This general atmosphere of futility is pervasive. Pessimists are usually steady in their pessimism; they tend not to see positive events as signposts to change their views.

Pessimism in the workplace can be learned behaviour, especially if the person in charge displays pessimistic tendencies.

We all like to get on well with our superiors and are keen not to do things which we know they'll dislike. We can then fall prey to a pattern of conformity in which we know that the boss hates risk, so we never suggest anything risky to him. Perhaps this is a peculiarly British phenomena, and our national character values steadiness in relationships, not putting yourself forward and blending in much more than it values disruptive innovation, even if it is more efficient.

Leadership has a profound effect on the culture of an organisation. If you encounter this level of pessimism and fear of failure in repeated attempts to engage with a body, it is likely due to cultural factors and the atmosphere created by leaders. Solutions are not easy in such situations. One option is to pick your moment, save your breath for a change in leadership when the systems is more open to new ideas, and less familiar with previous failures. Targeting your engagement to someone who has influence over the agenda-setters in an organisation but is open to the possibility of success is also useful. However, the most powerful tool is concrete evidence of other's success.

Fresh ideas

When a system is overwhelmed by the cloud of failure, it needs new and fresh thinking to draw it out of its malaise. Often the third sector is the source of such ideas. Early stage innovators can afford to take risks, embrace failure as part of the process and then scale up successful interventions.

Good ideas need to be proven. Social entrepreneurs can demonstrate the effectiveness of their ideas through controlled trials. The development economist Jeffrey Sachs considers the emergence of microcredit as a poverty reduction tool to be indicative of this trend, but it also shows us the dangers of a good idea being embraced by parties with the wrong motives.

"The idea is that by lending to small groups rather than to

individuals, collateral can be replaced by trust and group enforcement, since the group monitors its own members and ensures repayment. .... Making credit available to previously non-creditworthy micro-scale entrepreneurs enabled those people to break the trap of low income, low saving and low investment"[14]

Success at a small level lead to ramping up of involvement in micro-credit. It moved beyond auspices of the development charities into the mainstream financial world. Various investment houses were quick to jump on the bandwagon, setting up funds to provide private capital to the microcredit institutions which make the loans. However, something of a backlash is now emerging. The feted Mohammed Yunnus, Nobel Peace Prize winner, has been ejected from Grameen Bank. Stories of mis-selling of micro-loans, high interest rates and coercion have begun to emerge. It is an interesting case study on how public opinion can shift, but for now it suffices to say that you cannot rest on your laurels. A few high profile failures can taint your positive example; the reputational element needs to be carefully managed.

Slow and steady wins the race

We have seen how the dynamics of past failure, weak feedback and collective amnesia can create endlessly repeated cycles of failure, or lack of attempts at anything new. Underlying the collective pessimism and sense of futility embodied in any attempt to change things is a mis-match between what we imagine changes and success should look like, and what it actually looks like in real life. This has a great deal to do with time horizons, and our feeling that long-term gradual change is less valuable than disruptive, immediate success. Looking again at the end of slave trade we see how change came in a slow unfolding narrative, made possible by the indefatigable patience and sheer bloody-mindedness of men like Wilberforce.

Not only had the abolitionists decided to focus on the trade in slaves rather than the principle of slavery itself, thereby dodging a much more nuanced and difficult to win debate, the means of undermining the trade first came with some creative legislation. Using the war with France as a pretext, James Stephen suggested an innovative strategy to Wilberforce which would undermine the practice of most British ships to sail under neutral flags. The Foreign Slave Trade Bill made it illegal for British ships to deal in slaves under non-British flags, in 1806. Its effect was limited, but marked a gradual acceptance of the arguments, hidden in the purpose of curtailing trade with an enemy of the Empire.

Even the ultimate success of the British campaign belies the immediate reality. While trade with the British Colonies ceased, other countries' efforts to build economies on the back of slavery continued. The slave trade as a whole continued to grow during the heroic struggles of Wilberforce, Clarkson and Buxton. "Slave populations expanded, especially in Cuba, Brazil and the US[15]". However, the British effort was not in vein. It had proved that a major world power could not only muster the political will to enact such a change, but also that such efforts would not lead an entire nation to penury. It proved an example for the rest of the world, a vital weapon in the hands of abolitionists globally.

Calibration and Feedback

Learning from our mistakes is not a shiny new theory. It forms part of the most basic education we all receive, but we fail to appreciate its depth through our familiarity . We all undertake such processes in our daily domestic and professional lives. It makes sense at a gut level because we all use the reasoning to improve our performance in a given area, but the process has also been studied by behavioural psychologists. The simple process of learning from previous attempts at a goal which were unsuccessful form part of what we might call our 'adaptive toolbox' of ways of making better decisions. I hesitate to mention the arcane and unfathomable realm of cricket (for American readers - think baseball but with infinitely superior refreshments), but in this very English pastime I am a very average medium pace swing bowler. My aim as a I run up is to hit a particular spot on the cricket pitch, in order to maximise my chances of hitting the stumps. Before I let the ball go, I intend for it to move from left to right through the air, but I do not know how much it will move, since this depends on a whole number of extra factors, not least the atmospheric conditions and my ability to execute the skill of releasing the ball in the right position. Let's say - and this is not too far from reality - my first ball starts outside the off stump, and then swings in a glorious parabola from left to right, past the batsmen, past the wicket keeper and all the way to the boundary for an embarrassing four wides.

It's what I do next time that is crucial. I now know how much the ball will swing, so I adjust my initial aim to compensate. Starting the ball further to the left, the ball performs its heroics, this time shifting from left to right with unerring accuracy, honing in a rearranging the stumps. I might call this trial and error. A psychologist calls it 'feedback and qualitative causal modelling', which has a certain caché I'm sure you'll agree. This rationality of learning is most useful since it is done *after* an event or an attempt. The only way to guarantee failure to achieve a goal is to never try. A first attempt at dealing with a problem or issue is better seen not as a failure, but as a calibration which will help all subsequent actions be better attuned to goals we are trying to achieve.

How many times do millionaires try and fail before being successful in business? In any situation in which I am proficient, it is less due to pre-existing natural abilities, and more to do with a dedicated pursuit of a goal, in which I learn from my mistakes. If I know for sure what didn't work last time, I can be more confident that my remaining options will have a chance of working out. We all behave like this in our personal lives, but transferring this understanding to the workplace or organisational context can prove tricky. The role of leadership is vital here, since they create the culture where mistakes are either punished or welcomed as necessary calibrations. The sense of management wanting staff to be allowed to fail needs to be pervasive and go right through the organisation, however. Even if you are convinced that failure helps you ultimately succeed, you won't encourage it if your boss will castigate you for the failures of your department[16].

Repeating our mistakes

Learning from our mistakes is something we all like to think we are good at. But a quick look at an average relationship track record will indicate otherwise. You will encounter the odd person who is a spectacular failure in every area of life, but its more usual for people to have issues and weaknesses in one or two areas which they continually revisit. Learning from failure in these areas is hard, because it depends on strong feedback. When we are to blame, we are very poor at giving ourselves useful, balanced feedback.

Why is this? Let's take the case of a failed business venture. The entrepreneur in question tried to set up a business which struggled along for a couple of years, before finally and suddenly tanking. Asking this entrepreneur why he failed will likely not be very helpful, as he may well fall prey to what is termed by psychologists the 'fundamental attribution error'. When we look back, we attribute all negative events to bad luck and outside forces - the global economy, cheating staff, unhelpful bank manager. However, we treat all positive events as being the result of our personal talent, motivation and hard work.[17] An analysis of the reasons for business failures shows that our perceptions do not match reality. While most people would think that economic depression would be a major cause, the stats show otherwise, as it is possible for businesses to thrive in recessions (without ignoring the economic effects of job losses, of course). The more common causes are neglect - either through over ambition leading to people being overstretched, or lack of trust meaning nothing is delegated, resulting in trouble when the one individual around which every-thing revolves is out of action for some reason.

Repeated failure doesn't *always* create an increased likelihood of success for our next attempt, mainly because the failure and the negative emotion attached to it will undermine our motivation to try and deal with the problem again. This is true even when the decision itself is entirely rational, but acting on it would involve personal cost or an investment of time and energy.

Consider a smoker who is well aware of the health risks, has a clear knowledge that giving up their addiction to cigarettes is the right thing to do for themselves and their family, but having been convinced of this state of affairs, has yet to embark on the difficult process of giving up the habit. Habits are something we'll explore a little more in the next chapter, but it bears mentioning here that negative behavioural patterns can become habitually entrenched as well as positive ones. Our smoker may have found the initial motivation to give up, and tried to cut down. Perhaps he or she even managed to stop for a while. But the cravings, the physical symptoms of loss, the exclusion from the social group of 'the smokers' at the office or the pub and just the sheer difficulty of making changes in your personal life lead them to give up. Suppose they have tried many times, and failed. They feel worthless, weak willed and powerless. Hence they know exactly what the rational decision is, but the personal costs to them from their chosen method of giving up leave them trapped in a cycle of behaviour which is damaging their health.

You can't really argue with someone in this situation. They are convinced of the causal relationship, and that something should be done to break the cycle, but they are hopeless to see how they can make such changes. Motivation, such as it was, has been eroded by repeated failure. Their perceptions of reality may well have been distorted also - they may longer trust advice given by healthcare professionals, for example. Dealing with someone or some organisation trapped in these negative cycles may involve some restating of the factual arguments if the weight of them has been lost. It may be that the person has forgotten that they are on a destructive path, and some negative coercion will be effective. But more successful work can be done to convince somebody that new tools, better ways of dealing with the problem and new strategies exists for them to have a much better chance of succeeding if they have another go.

Theoretically, their previous failure should show them what does and doesn't work for them. Analysing the reasons for the failure are therefore key. If the smoker found the physical symptoms too hard to deal with, the nicotine patches and chewing gum could help. If it was the social aspect, the perhaps a support group or a starting a new hobby as a displacement activity could help. A few pages ago we discussed my thought processes as I seek to improve my performance within in a friendly game of cricket. Your first attempt to quit was like my first ball of the over - a spectacular failure which set you up for spectacular success the next time, if only you'd try again. If you have encountered such road blocks of despair borne of failure, then it might be time for a 'softer' approach, providing comfort and words of affirmation that change is indeed possible.

From despair to hope

The power of a successful example is under-appreciated. In the 1950's, in the entire span of human history no man had run a mile in under 4 minutes. The finest athletes of generations had tried and failed; it was as good as impossible. Then one man broke the 4 minute mile, and within a year, several others had broken it too. Many of us are not pioneers, but we are well capable of much more than we give ourselves credit for. Perhaps those runners who broke the 4 minute barrier later were not capable of striving for the impossible, and had stopped trying to reach it.

But once the signal came from Roger Bannister that it breaking 4 minutes could be done, I imagine that training efforts re-doubled, as the awareness of greatness trickled down, suggesting that they could indeed push themselves harder and faster, since 4 minutes for a mile was now possible. Slipstreaming is a social as well as a physical phenomenon.

In business and public discourse this holds true also. The inventor is often not the one who makes a success of the idea. Apple has perfected this approach in recent years - redefining the personal music player, the personal computer and the smart phone, despite being relative late comers to all of these markets. Once a base market has been established, and the market drivers identified, they set about bringing excellence and beauty to the masses. Rarely do they create innovations - but they excel at integrating existing technologies in easy to use pretty packages. Tablet computers had been around for years before Apple got involved. When they did, they changed everything. Now everybody sees that tablet computers are a market that they want a piece of, benefitting from Apple's spectacular success. If you are encountering excuses of past failure, you need to recognise these different roles - do you need a pioneer or an establisher? Do you need to blaze a trail, or widen one? Both are equally valid options.

The compromiser who makes the best use of this excuse taps into the hidden reserves of self-doubt and guilt that we all try and hide from our peers. If he can make you painfully aware of the risks of failing again, he can be reasonably sure you won't be bothering him for a long time with your nagging to do things differently. Reframing the debate, displaying a vision of appropriate diagnosis of the problem and infusing the process with verve and positive examples can get enough people on your side to set things up for another try.

All of this is easier when the place reeks of failure. But what about a much more comfy compromiser, whose patterns are established so that everyone who matters is happy?

Chapter 3

But we've always done it that way

My friend Ben looked perturbed. He had set off for a little run on the San Diego coastline, leaving me to mind the surfboards. As he set off, he gradually become aware that he was being followed by a middle aged man with sun glasses and a toned, tanned physique. As Ben, ever the Brit, slowed down to let him overtake, the man slowed down with him. He then sped up, and the man matched him. The man then proclaimed "Hey, we run at the same speed, you and me! My name's Rhett". Rhett then preceded to talk at my friend for the next ten minutes about the benefits of forming habits. If you do something new for 30 days, you'll keep doing it. It also had something to do with trying to get Ben to join his gym. Presumably he has formed the habit of stalking tourists on beaches over a period of longer than thirty days.

A minor incident in an otherwise uneventful holiday, but the line has stayed with me. Just how do habits become established, and can we get into habits as organisations?

This is the last of the psychological and behavioural traits displayed by humans which can be exploited as excuses for inaction by the comfortable compromiser. In practically every situation where you are suggesting change, it is reasonable to assume that there is previous existing practice which you wish to challenge. Where does this one-size-fits-all excuse for everything gain its universal character from? Mainly that we are dealing with systems which are the product of years of evolution, a mixture of fast and slow growth. As such, we'll necessarily have to summarise a great deal of information from a wide range of fields of study if we are to begin to understand the roots of this excuse.

Steady on!

The simplicity of an established approach is not always the root of its downfall. Just because someone relies on habits and doesn't consider every single piece of information coming their way doesn't mean that they are making the 'wrong' decision or making a poor choice. There may be one one indicator which we really need to pay attention to, and having paid attention to it, we have created a shortcut to making a decision. The simplifying techniques we use to make decisions like this - on *appropriately* limited sets of information - are called 'heuristics', a term you can use to impress your friends at dinner parties. Understanding the usefulness of our habits is an important starting point for understanding how this excuse is used.

There is no one established, complete theory of heuristics, but some crude distinctions can be made. We have three general classes of these decision aiding rules. First, simple search rules, methods of looking for information which are repeated as necessary. Second, simple stopping rules, determining when the search stops, usually when the first option which fits our search criteria is found (the first - not necessarily the best). And thirdly, simple decision rules; once some information has been found and the search has been stopped, we make a decision based on one very important reason or criteria. The crucial observation is not just that these decisions can be made without some huge calculation of all the pros and cons, weighing up the probabilities of the likelihood of various benefits coming our way, but that those decisions can be useful *despite* their being incomplete. The 'way we've always done things' might seem to be superficial, but this does not stop it being adequate and appropriate.

Two academics working in the field of heuristics, Gigerenzer and Selten, use the example of a robot constructed to catch a 'high ball' to illustrate this point, and the fact that simpler approach is not always problematic.[18] Human baseball and cricket players have developed a core skill of catching high balls.

Building a robot to perform this task, we imagine two different teams of engineers. The first team takes as its starting point all the possible paths of balls which can be hit towards its robot. The robot has the instruments it needs to decide which parabola the ball is travelling along. These parabolas are programmed in, but they may be affected by spin and wind. So the robot needs more instruments to track the spin, analyse it, and compute its effect on the path of the ball. Using these detailed measurements, a powerful computer will do all the calculations, and produce an estimate of where the ball will land, move the robot to this point, and catch it.

Another team of engineers uses a shortcut. They begin with studying what actual baseball players or cricketers do (an option dismissed by the other team as being subjective and unconscious, and therefore unmeasureable). Using this cue, they programme the robot to use the first half second of its programmed task to do a rough calculation of whether the ball will land in front of or behind it. It will then be programmed to start moving forward or back, fixing its focus on the ball. It then is programmed to adjust its speed to keep the angle between the ball and its 'gaze' remains constant. It will catch the ball.

The difference is huge. Both robots catch the ball, but one pays attention to a single informational cue, the angle of gaze, which acts as an effective shortcut to the consideration of spin, wind and drag.[19] The 'full rationality' robot is a complicated and advanced machine, created with the capacity to perform vast numbers of calculations based on a huge number of information inputs. The other is simple and elegant, and much cheaper and simpler to operate. As the researchers summarise, 'simplicity ... can enable fast, frugal, and accurate decisions'.

However, such shortcuts and rules of thumb operate since they exploit a key characteristic in a given environment. They work because one constant or relationship between factors acts as a short-cut, an indicator for a number of equally important criteria. In the catching robots, the angle of gaze constant does not remove the need to consider spin, drag and wind, but rather acts as a simple proxy for it. Elegant problem solving solutions can be found without exhaustive enquiry, but they are not general in character. Therefore, established rules of thumb are often very context specific. You have reason to challenge someone's over-reliance on 'the way I've always done things" firstly if they are transposing their established practices from very different situations, but also if those situations in which they are developed are changing.[20]

Of course, the fastest and cheapest way of adapting to a new situation is to copy someone else. Humans have evolved to mimic observed successful behaviours, since it enables people to make advances without having to go through all the trial and error themselves. This is true as we observe our children growing up, learning successful behaviours for feeding and surviving from their parents, but also happens in business. One way of training new staff is to have them 'sit next to Nellie' - by sitting next to the person who has already learned the job, they copy not just the basics of the task but all the effective shortcuts and opportunities to cut corners. At a wider level in business, if someone else is undercutting your business model with a new method of production, you could struggle unless you adapted by copying them (if you keep it legal, of course!). However, imitation has its dangers. You may have adopted someone else's established practice, but also their inefficiencies. This can lead to an entire industry using sub-optimal procedures, but since we've all 'always done it that way', there is little appetite for change.

We don't need anything new

The same can apply to ideas as well as behaviours. When an issue becomes the subject of continued debate within society, especially when it is an issue which lacks the hard edges of timescales, budgetary limits and the like, policy tends to evolve and be added to rather than be taken away. If you are beginning to move in an area which not only has established practice but a concurrent history of other attempts to shift it, you will face an argument along these lines: "We don't need anything new - what we need is proper enforcement of what laws on the topic we already have".

The debate on gun control in America is set up exactly on these lines, as people can point to thousands of regional and national regulations which are not adequately enforced. But such thinking is a little lazy, and ignores the need for progressive implementation which actually achieves useful changes. In essence, what the country needs is 'better gun laws, not more guns'. If the policy in place is flawed in some fundamental way, it is a waste of time and resources to try and implement it, no matter how 'used' to the laws you are (Vizzard).

Removing established procedures and challenging the "we've always done it that way" excuse isn't just about addressing someone's fear of embracing the new, facing more work in order to implement new systems or fearing failure. It's also about the fear of an emerging new situation which the old system could have handled, but the new one couldn't. The perceived danger is that you will be left embarrassed if you change something, and then disaster strikes.

Airline security is a case in point, as we've already seen. The various additional procedures and systems which have been implemented in the aftermath of 9/11 don't really match the risks we face from global terrorism today. There are several compelling reasons to suggest that an incident like 9/11 is very unlikely, as is the prospect of commercial airlines continuing to be a target[21]. Security measures doesn't move with the risk entailed, but seem to be an infinitely expanding list of require-ments, much to the chagrin of the airline industry. Regulators are demonstrating a form of paranoia about the future, in which they are loathe to scale back or remove any security requirement lest it be exploited in a future terrorist attack. They are at desperate pains to avoid being the people who 'dropped the ball' and allowed another 9/11. When dealing with risk, and public safety, it is far harder to argue for something to be taken away than to be added, since someone will always be identified historically with the change.

Failing to adapt

Doing things the way we've always done them is dangerous when it represents a failure to adapt to a new situation, one where our established behaviours are leading us down a dangerous path. If our argument for change has come up against this failure to adapt, then we probably need to understand what causes it before we can hope to engage someone in a debate about the necessity of them changing their minds about the need for change. What causes people to use the wrong strategy in relation to a problem, or to use the right one in an inappropriate way?

The causes are indistinct, but divisible into two general classes[22]. Firstly, and rather obviously, the lack of adaptivity may be based on a lack of information. You may not know enough about the situation, your options or the likely effects of your different decisions. Second, you may fail to execute the strategy well. Your role will change depending on the particular lack of adaptivity you identify. Taking climate change as an example, certain groups appear to have adopted a certain ideologically rooted ignorance to the necessity for adaptation to the problem. They are failing to adapt since they are not willing to even accept new information. Second, they may have know about the problem, and decided on a course of action - a cap and trade system, for example - but they lack confidence to execute the strategy well enough. Having identified the root of the excuse, you can decide which personality to adopt in order to engage effectively. Perhaps you will be an advocate and educator, or maybe a mothering figure, holding their hand and reassuring them that you're there to help execute the strategy.

The risk of relying on out-dated wisdom

Our preference for relying on what we've always done assumes that we can in fact make logical, rational and complete decisions based on perfect evaluation of perfect information. I would not describe any decision I have ever made as attaining to this standard, let alone the companies or organisation that I have worked with and for. Established practice may be seen as the only way to go, since it makes the most sense in the moment, and it has worked before.

However, our inbuilt tendency to stick with our established way of doing something persists even when there might be better ways of achieving the same goal. Once we learn a skill, or a method, we develop a confidence in it which is sometimes misplaced. A famous experiment by Abraham and Edith Luchins proves this point.

The subjects of the study were given a maths problem involving various containers which held different amounts of water. They were asked to get a specified amount of water by using the cups of different volumes. By adding and subtracting amounts of water using the quantities allowed, it was possible to arrive at the goal. Most people found the challenge initially tough, but soon got the hang of it. Crucially, they found a particular pattern was successful in all of the challenges they were given.

It gets interesting when the tinkering began. The same subjects were given a different set of containers where the pattern they had learned would work, but there was also a much simpler solution available. A very high proportion (between 64% and 83%) continued to use the complex procedure they knew worked rather than reconsider the possibility of a simpler one. The second experiment was conducted with a fresh set of subjects, and 95-99% of them spotted the new, easier way of getting to the goal.

This sounds as a warning to us against complacency. Just because 'we've always done it that way' doesn't mean it's still the best thing to do; new and better solutions may be right in front of us, but our established habits and patterns don't let us see them. Life, however, rewards risk takers. If the best available option and the established practice would only give you limited reward since you are constrained by the situation, then it's worth considering making a risky move which would open up new possibilities.

Studies of the decision making behaviour of human chess grandmasters compared with the best computer programmed players expose this fact. A chess game is a very useful context in which to study the way in which human beings make decisions. Not only is the context more fixed than real life (in that the only real variable is the behaviour and next move of your opponent, since the number of pieces, their abilities and the end game are fixed), but the better chess players will have been dedicated students of previous players' moves and theories on strategy. Chess players do not evaluate their available options in a given situation one by one, weighing up the benefits of one move against each other, according to a core set of criteria. They don't sit down and ask themselves "which move will protect my king the best?". Instead, they have been observed to make comparisons at a much more general level, looking at the way the game might pan out were they to make the move they are considering. They will look at what opportunities they may get from making a move, discount some as worthless or boring, identify a few options, and then make a decision based on some weighting. But the overall strategy is one of a general feel for future opportunities. Interestingly, when faced with pressure, players make rather different decisions. If a player is behind, he will likely make a decision which is riskier, but opens up a whole new world of possibilities.

Computer players have often lacked this imaginative response to adversity. They will continue to make rational choices of pre-programmed options based on a list of criteria. When they are behind, they remain conservative, trying to protect the king. The best human players will adapt all of their past learning, realise they have a limited chance of victory if they continue with these strategies, and risk a loss which is looking increasingly likely for the sake of opening up the possibility of new scenarios in which they win.

In our organisations, we can begin to feel a little bit like a pre-programmed computer. Our compliance teams and regulatory exams force us into a way of thinking which is very unimaginative - in many cases rightly so. If your job involves looking after peoples' money or making things which need to be well made to be safe, we don't really want you to be too creative. However, the addiction to following established practice when you are behind in 'the game' limits your possibilities to win. The chess master is a master learner, developing the skill of balancing his options to create a narrative in which he may win. The computer does maths, and makes calculations. If I had to choose one to play for my soul in a chess match against Death, I know which one I would choose.

Habits are comfortable

Having seen that observable proof that habits can sometimes deceive, we must ask why we place so much trust in established practice. Humans maintain a preference for things that we understand, and things we have encountered previously. If a situation at work presents itself to us and we have dealt with similar situations easily in the past, we will probably default to using that method. We've always done it that way, so why waste time considering other options, if the one we pursue is good enough?

One of the purest and most simple kinds of decision we can

make is between two alternative courses of action. Assuming that the only information we have to hand is our past experience with the alternatives, we will likely choose the alternative with which we have some experience over the other. We can 'do little better than rely on our **partial ignorance,** choosing recognised options over unrecognised ones'.[23] The way we've always done things is comfortable and familiar, and going with what we have experience of doing will usually yield better results than if we were to just select from the options at random. The nagging doubt that haunts us is the fear of wasting time. If we spend extra effort investigating the other possibility and it turns out to be less useful than the one we already know, no-one will thank us for delaying doing what would have worked already for the sake of some intellectual inquiry.

This recognition effect isn't just applicable to simple tasks. Taking an activity close to my heart, a great deal of research has been done into the behaviour of stock traders, and their employment of rules of thumb and internal guidelines in trying to decide which companies to invest in. Stock picking is a highly complex activity, with a much larger range of possibilities than we have considered above. Vast amounts of information feed into the trader's systems, so vast as to need the best and the brightest minds to run the mathematical models which help to make sense of the data. Each trader will have developed a reliance on a particular set of rules for making decisions - only picking stocks with high exposure to certain markets, not picking companies with dividends which are not well covered by profits, for example. Within an individual team, these rules may be shared, but taken across the market, a vast number of different and contrasting rules will be employed by traders and paid for by clients.

Habits are like comfort blankets which use to insulate ourselves from a complex and difficult world. This observation helps our understanding of the enshrinement of "the way we've always done things" in organisational behaviour.[24] Continuing to deal with investment, we are looking at a highly complicated decision making environment. The likelihood that our successful rules are properly rational is therefore low. What is more likely is that our rules developed through misinterpretation of causes in a company's success or failure, or through false correlations - much in the same way that basic superstitions persist even in the most 'rational' people. Secondly, in the face of a scarily complex and seemingly volatile environment which can reward you handsomely or leave you penniless in the course of one day in the market, it's surely more comforting to have some system to rely on than nothing at all. All of this results in a slightly uncomfortable conclusion; our increased knowledge and reasoning capacity may make us more likely to adopt such short-cuts them, not less!

Further, we tend to place what is pre-existing in time in a more favourable light due to the sub-conscious processes of 'anchoring'. This is a well observed phenomena in the psychological study of negotiation. It involves a cognitive bias towards the first standard we are presented with, against which all other suggestions or adjustments are judged in the negotiation. So, in the case of valuing goods for sale, people are influenced by guide prices at a very deep level. 'Asking prices' act as convenient 'anchors'. But goals may just as easily be 'anchors' which affect our ability to reason and negotiate in the argument. That is not to say that we don't know our own mind, or what our limits are, but to point out that the first price or goal mentioned might not be the most appropriate for the discussion at hand.

Established practice and the benefits and risks it brings act as the 'framing' for a debate. The way we've always done things acts as our anchor for understanding our approach to an issue, often creating the opportunity for new and better approaches to be misunderstood or missed entirely. There is a danger in established procedures become the standard against which subsequent adjustments are made. The choice of anchor - the initial offer in a negotiation, say, or the initial attempt to deal with a problem - may 'be based on faulty or incomplete information and thus be misleading in and of itself'. But once it's defined, people tend to treat it as real.

Our framing and anchoring changes our appetite for risk. We behave very differently when we are looking to gain something as opposed to avoid losing something. If an offer is seen in your mind as resulting in a loss, you will likely be more willing to take risks for a better deal. If the offer is a gain, you will be less likely to want to risk losing the offer entirely. This is important. You might react very differently to a perceived loss than to a perceived gain. As Lewicki observes, "When negotiators are risk averse, they are more likely to accept any viable offer simple because they are afraid of losing. In contrast, when negotiators are risk seeking, they are likely to wait for a better offer or for future concessions."[25]

Taking an example from private negotiation, prior commitment to an idea or proposal can be very 'sticky' and difficult to dislodge, further explaining people's preference for maintaining the 'way we've always done it'. Once we have decided on something, usually after some commitment of time and energy to the process, we are unusually persistent and consistent in our beliefs. Advertisers have long understood the power of a prior commitment. We see an advertisement through a website for an excellent deal on Hi-Fi speakers. We decide this is a good deal and that we intend to buy the speakers, and we drive to the store. On arrival, we find the store has run out of speakers at the deal price, but there are some slightly better, slightly more expensive speakers on offer. Once we've decided on buying speakers, and committed internally to spending money, lots of us will buy the speakers, even at a price which would not have induced us to come to the store in the first place. Such is the power of a commitment to a course of action; it can lead us into decisions which we would not make if the facts were presented to us in a different way.

Understanding commitment is important in dealing with the argument in question. We need to have a real understanding of the other party's commitment to the established order, not just what they gain under it. Conversely, getting small agreements can be a way of inching someone away from their entrenched position. If you can't get some to agree that a whole system needs changing, focus on a sub-set of the system which is particularly dysfunctional and try to get agreement on that. Creating a sense of mutual commitment will open up the other party to making future deals with you.

Habits can kill

They might be useful, and occasionally comforting, but we all know that habits can be formed even when they are dangerous and cause us harm. Humans can develop physical and psychological addictions to alcohol and other stimulants. We can become numb to the damage being done, and we keep smoking or drinking despite the damage it is doing us. National and International politicians can behave in a similarly addicted way, repeatedly implementing policies which we know are damaging.

The structural adjustment era of the 1980s and the set of economic reforms imposed on developing countries to liberalise their markets and reduce trade barriers was the established paradigm. Yet even when its negative effects were being felt, it remained established practice. The development economist Susan George argues that it doesn't matter how many mistakes mainstream economists make since they are 'protected and nurtured by those whose political objectives they support, package and condone, they have a licence to go on making them, whatever the consequences'. When we are faced with the 'pushing of a paradigm', even when it is obviously causing more harm than intended, she suggests that the battle ground is not ideology but accountability, sound advice for our purposes. In development economics, the right course of action was not to develop new a radical ideas to supplant the existing paradigm (although this is necessary), but to make sure mainstream economic policies were rigorously assessed and those who pushed them held to account for the damage they caused. Those who push the paradigm 'go on getting their comfortable salaries no matter how much human suffering their policies demonstrably cause. They are not subject to ostracism by their peers. They continue to dominate the 'respectable' publications and the institutions where those who will follow in their footsteps will be trained. They are not accountable.'[26]

In business circles, the story is told of a factory refit in which the workers 'did what we've always done', with hilarious consequences. The factory in question had in the past operated a back-up generator in the basement of its facility. The steam pipes for the rest of the plant were directed around this generator. The generator was removed, as the factory had found other emergency power sources. When the pipes came to be refitted, they copied what was there already - sending the new pipes in a circuitous route to avoid a generator which was no longer there. They were just doing what they had always done - but ended up looking ridiculous, failing appreciate the changes in circumstance before their eyes, or indeed the function and purpose of what they were doing.

George Orwell once stated that "first duty of intelligent men is the restatement of the obvious". This can be a frustrating step for many, but in some cases is vital to avoid making a mistake which has implications for the rest of the entire project. In the case of the factory, someone should have asked - what is the pipe for, and why does it bend? You might do well to start with such elementary questions, and then ask them of the opposition.

Knowing when to call an experiment a failure is impossible to get exactly right. The best we can possibly hope for is to have thought about the problems before hand, set up the right monitoring mechanisms to look for the right indicators of success *and* failure, and be honest with ourselves in the assessment of the 'facts' which we then gather. We can convince ourselves that next time will be different, or that the opponents will least expect us to do exactly what we did last time[27].

Decisions, decisions

Exploring some basic theories of decision making will help us to understand why and how the same mistakes seem to be made in succession, and how we might feel that our solution is obvious whereas the person making the mistake cannot see it. Firstly, some policy science thinkers take a rational view of the way in which we make decisions (Ham & Hill 1993). That is, they posit that we sum up our available options and make a choice between them based on our projection of what will best for us or our organisation, based on a knowledge of our values. Except knowing everything about everything is difficult. So we tend, in the real world, to reduce the amount of information, alternatives and consequences down into a manageable amount of choices using rules of thumb and convention. Herbert Simon coined the term 'bounded rationality' to describe this process, since we take a subset of a seemingly infinite set of choices, and make a rational decision within that boundary.

It's easy to see how you may repeat mistakes given this context, since you might not ever think about potential new solutions for your problem. However, it doesn't stop there. Working on Simon's theory, Charles Lindblom suggested that it gets worse, since we actually make *successive* bounded and limited comparisons and policy decisions. In practice, decision making is often incremental. It may seem inadequate, but is more realistic than assuming that all decisions are made knowing everything about everything, what Lindbolm described as a 'futile attempt at superhuman comprehensiveness'.[28] The best we can do is 'muddle through more effectively'.[29] The estab-lished ways and patterns are a result of a gradual progression of limited choices and data sets. Your new idea may be just the alter-native they've been looking for, but their development and cumulative effect of years of 'bounded' choices may have limited their thinking.

Understanding our 'path dependency'

I feel the need to introduce a little bit of balance at this point. It is not easy to change things; that isn't the point of this chapter. The main concept I'm trying to hammer home is that change is always possible, even if it would be hard. However, I am a realist, and we have to know what stops people from changing things before we effectively address their concerns and worries. I also know that some things persist which are not just dumb habits.

In international development, many interesting and novel ideas have been produced and tested, showing the possibility of better ways of managing a society, socially and economically. Implementing these ideas is not always easy. This is due to the process of change, and how it happens. It's rare for massive, seismic changes to be seen; when they do occur, the impacts on citizens are immense - countries struggle to develop quickly following intense periods of civil war, coup d'états and regime change. Instead, most societal change is gradual, the sum effect of millions of smaller decisions. Un-picking this web of rules, regulations, decisions and compromises, rewinding society back to a point where we can implement new ideas is incredibly challenging. We have gone so far down a path, it's hard to imagine backing up to the crossroads in order to try something new. Our future is dictated by our past. This, in simple terms, is called 'path dependency'[30]. Theorists in the field of social science refer to it as 'institutional stickiness' - where those in charge fail to respond to the changing the environment, even when there are better ways of doing things available to them.

The term has gained wide acceptance, but is in danger of becoming a fatalistic belief. It's now akin to a collective sigh, summing up our belief that we can't really change things, since the sub-optimal situation we find ourselves in is actually pretty stable, a comfortable compromise. We can't apparently trust ourselves to right our wrongs, not to make the same mistakes over and over again. Situations which are just about effective can persist, even when there might be many better potential outcomes. A good example is the location of a business. If in the past we needed to power our operations by using a water wheel, we needed to be near a fast flowing river, Now, we power our machines using electricity but we have invested millions in our factory by the river. To move away to better facilities is difficult to conceive. Or the decision may not have been rational in the first place. We may have located our facility here just because others did, and we didn't really plan for the future but follow the heard. Our future is dictated by decisions made in the past, not just by our habits!

However, the term as originally concocted is not fatalistic and actually explicitly imagines the existence of options between which we can choose. It sees different possible paths, but is concerned with why we are 'locked-in' to particular ones. Thankfully, the social scientists in the field have been quick to recognise the fatalism and many works are being produced suggesting ways to break the dependence, and produce effective change.

One source of hope to break fatalistic path dependency is fact is that most institutions are not operating at full capacity. They will be full of 'redundancies', that is, functional capabilities which are under used or under funded. They may have many hidden characteristics, abilities and skills which are not being used. Especially as institutions grow in size and complexity, their hidden abilities grow. The social scientists Ebbinghaus and Manow looked into the effectiveness of welfare states in Europe which had successfully reformed themselves despite apparent path dependencies, observing that 'they ceased to embody a simple logic, but (were) a complex bundle, dormant elements of which may open up possibilities for change at difficult moments'.[31] It is this element, the fact that human beings are capable of endless innovation if we are willing to lift our eyes from our own work, share it with and listen to that of others, which shines like a ray of light into the deterministic darkness.

"Buy more chairs"

I have seen first hand the full effect of such a 'Eureka' moment. The year following my graduation was spent working for a highly complex, intriguing and functional institution, an Evangelical non-denominational church of about 1,000 members. This was a profoundly eye-opening introduction into the world of work, not only in terms of my personal disciplines, but in the internal politics and the way change was conceived and managed.[32] My introduction to path dependency came with the regular ordeal of the Monday team meeting. The church was a rough hierarchy, consisting of three congregations each with their own leadership teams. I worked in the student ministry. On Monday we'd all get together, a real mix of people, roles and paradigms of change processes - pastors, administrative workers, caretakers and general dogsbodies such as myself. For the first few months I remember clearly one thing being discussed over and over, to the exclusion of other matters; the chairs.

Our building was an old church, which had seen use by a TV company as a prop store since falling into disrepair in the 1930's. It had multiple levels. Once a month we had a big youth gathering in our main hall, and shifted our evening service downstairs. To make this happen, we needed to move about 50-70 chairs down the stairs to the crypt area. I believe the technical term for this was a 'right palaver'. The chairs were bulky and heavy. We press ganged congregants hanging around for coffee after the morning service into grabbing a few chairs and taking them downstairs. This would have been simple, except that the children's church was just finishing downstairs, so you had the wonderful health and safety risk of middle aged men struggling with 8 plastic chairs in a stack trying to negotiate the narrow corridor in which 100 plus toddlers and parents were trying to ascend. Then, later on, you had to get another bunch of people to move the chairs BACK. It was the bane of our lives.

Every Monday with the pain of the chair faff fresh in our minds, we would discuss the chairs. Could we get a volunteer team together to move them? Could we find a better path to take the chairs downstairs? Could we install a one-way system so the kids went round the side of the building? At one point we even discussed the possibility of installing a lift in our listed building, at great costs, just to move the chairs.

After months of this, and no resolution, a friend who was also volunteering for the church finally broke. She said very little at these meetings. But her contribution on this occasion consisted of three words which solved the problem in a flash:

"BUY MORE CHAIRS!"

There was an embarrassed silence. We all looked at the floor, as the reality of this brilliantly simple idea, which had always been available to us, was made clear. Looking back, we were locked in; we thought the problem was how to move the chairs we already had. It took one person to step back, notice our path dependency and break it with a far more optimal outcome, achievable that day without great cost. One which a team of 20 plus people with a high degree of managerial and intellectual skill had failed to come up with in 4 months.

Our path dependency is reinforced by our specialities and disciplines. We can focus on being an expertise in a given field, narrowing our focus in for the sake of becoming a master of the detail. There is nothing implicitly wrong with this, but we must be aware that we have become restricted and narrow, and that our knowledge may have an explosive power is joined with another specialism from another discipline. To continue the shameless sociological name-dropping, Hollingsworth observed that those research and development institutions with a high degree of success seemed to excel in 'interdisciplinary and integrated activity across diverse fields of science'. Essentially, it's valuing the redundancy that such interdisciplinary creates now, based on the potential for game changing discoveries that it makes potentially possible in the future.

Of course, our expertise is not constrained to one field, and herein lies another opportunity to break away from path dependency. We all have multiple roles in society. I am a boyfriend, a housemate, and accountability partner, a company secretary, a board member, a brother, a son, a researcher, a writer, a trail runner, a musician and a gardener, to name but a few. I do not profess to possess expertise in all of these fields, but I certainly do in some, as you will in all the roles and responsibilities you have in your life. Every organisation is made up of many such people, every person carrying with them a world of knowledge and experience gleaned outside of their immediate context. If I am in one context which appears to be 'stuck', with no additional resource, with no new ideas, I can 'borrow' from my other contexts, suggesting radically different ideas which can be 'game changers'. Of course, they might just be silly ideas, and not work, but their beauty is in their potential.

The trick comes in creating the atmosphere and culture where all such ideas and skills have an opportunity to be expressed. Some people will be too opinionated about what is wrong and the way they think things should be done, and others with potentially brilliant ideas will never speak up, prefer to keep themselves to themselves and go home at 5pm every day. A good manager or change agent will harness both sets of energies and passions. There are many useful techniques which have developed to facilitate such discussions, but they all include the core elements of removing hierarchy, removing any potential for criticism or blame, and creating avenues for quieter people to be heard.

Even if we organise ourselves to remain open to new ideas, varied enough in our team roles to borrow examples of successful structures from other disciplines, and are generally aware of our tendency to get stuck on a particular path, we might not always have all the options available to us for one other reason. We are not in charge, and the person in authority withholds other options from us. We may have 'always done it this way' because the founder said so, or our middle manager wants it done that way. Identifying the existence of such constraints is therefore very important when you begin your study of the people you are trying to persuade.

Entrepreneurs and innovators do not operate outside of the tendency to develop path dependency. They do not, as is popularly imagined, come up with staggeringly unique and original ideas from 'outside'. Instead, they move along the paths developed by historical choices, but are aware of these constraints, making the decision to break from it where they see an opportunity. You don't want to reinvent the wheel, and some paths have become so well established precisely because they are excellent ways of meeting the needs which gave rise to the activities.[33]

Breaking free - creative solutions

The current situation may be so embedded that change would be highly complicated and labour intensive to bring about. The argument follows a familiar pattern in social regulation, as we see when we return to our consideration of gun control in the US. There is one very practical objection to attempts to restrict gun ownership, namely that a large number of Americans already own weapons. A 1999 federal government study found that 36% of households in the country had *at least* one gun. This is a supply problem - its no use regulating future supply if the existing supply is enough to give you considerable headaches. Prohibition suffered from the same problem. The amount of alcohol in the country did not disappear overnight, meaning there was ready supply of alcohol available to interested bootleggers.

Is this argument always powerful, that the physical 'facts on the ground' create a path dependency which is hard to break free of? That is, if you seek to change something which is already established, and where the physical assets embodying the problem are already widely dispersed, should you retreat into "the art of the possible" and seek to make changes around the fringe, incremental improvements which make marginal increases in welfare?

Some creative thinking would help. Taking the example of gun control, you may not be able to control the supply of firearms, since a large number of people either enjoy them for hunting or believe they will provide additional home security. It's never been tried (and it first came in to my mind via the subversive African American comedian, Chris Rock) but one way to intervene would be to restrict the supply of ammunition. Paraphrasing Mr Rock, if a bullet cost $5,000, people would think before they shot someone. There would be no more innocent bystanders; and in his world view, if someone shot you, you *must* have does something to deserve it since they spent a year's wages on the bullets they shot you with!

It's fatuous, but it demonstrates a point. If you can't change the level of penetration of a technology, then take a wider view and look at the supply chain. How is the service or product supplied, and what peripherals or additional supplies does it need to enable continued use? With ammunition, should it be available at Wal-Mart, or should it be available only through licensed dealers, with person quotas for use?

Shifting the burden of proof

We mentioned at the start of the first chapter that fundamental bias exists toward what we have been doing for years and we maintain a preference for dealing with problems that are familiar to us. Sometimes the comfortable compromiser will dictate from his positions of pre-eminence that *you* must mount an exhausting defence of your proposed change, while the existing paradigm continues unchallenged. Israel Zangwill, novelist and playwright, a pro-suffrage supporter in the early twentieth Century, gives us an example of a very useful strategy; shift the burden of proof onto your opposition;

> "The proposition we are here to maintain is so simple, so clear, that when one is called upon to justify it, one scarcely knows what to say. The fact is, it is not our business to justify it; the onus of proof lies on the other side. How do they justify their monstrous proposition that one half of the human race shall have no political rights? When Wilberforce started his campaign against slavery, it was scarcely Wilberforce's business to defend the proposition that no man has the right to make a chattel of another. The burden of proof lies on the slave-owner. Our case is, I say, so simple, that it is like having to prove that one and one are two."[34]

Often the establishment has long persisted in a stance without recent reassessment of its legitimacy. It is insufficient to defend something because 'we've always done it that way'. While there may have been good reason to have adopted that stance in the past, the facts may have changed.

Understanding our relationship to the past and the future

These first three chapters have dealt with excuses relating to the way in which we conceptualise the effects of actions on our futures, in comparison to the current and past scenarios. It stems from a unique characteristic of human beings and human society – namely that we are able to imagine the future and work back from this conception to inform our present decisions and actions. This ability is seen by some as a reflection of our basic ability at the cellular level to appreciate what is around us, and interact with our environment accordingly. All cellular organisms do this to a greater or lesser extent, but human beings have developed a conceptual ability to process and analyse their environment and change current behaviour in accordance with an imagined future reality. We do not live purely as creatures of instinct, but as creatures of society, where discussion and the swapping of ideas form a strong part of decision making process.

In looking at failure and resistance to change, we have assumed that change will always be a good thing, and assumed that all arguments against it are merely excuses. But the section would not be complete without some acknowledgement that change is not always helpful or useful. The problem comes in when we consider that the very thought of change is an attractive one, even when the established way of doing things is probably the best way, or at least is efficient enough not to warrant much tinkering. In recent election cycles in the US and UK, the language of change was used widely. You couldn't be on a ticket if you didn't offer some kind of change - be it "change we can believe in" or "time for change".

And what of the apparent intractability of certain problems? Can some controversies in fact never be resolved, in which case the search for new alternatives is futile? Debates such as abortion are incredibly difficult, with battle lines drawn on sacred ground. That the debate is hard is no surprise; but the conclusion may be challenged - are such moral debates inherently un-resolvable? That an argument is hard to resolve is not a unique feature of a moral argument - some factual arguments are just as hard. We think of conspiracy theorists, insisting that the moon landings were faked despite evidence to the contrary. You may just have the misfortune to be dealing with an awkward, difficult person who really doesn't want to agree with you or anyone else. It may be that the issue in question is clouded in scientific uncertainty, with inconclusive evidence on either side.

It is important to take a long-term perspective. If you have been dealing with a hard issue day in day out for years, you may be emotionally and intellectually exhausted, despairing of every reaching a conclusion to the moral wrestling match you are part of. Human history should offer some hope, however. Because we hear the most about the most difficult issues, we tend to assume that they are more intractable than they really are; but if you could talk to someone from the 18th Century and tell them that slavery had been abolished, would they believe you? Part of the point of this book is to reaffirm to an increasingly apathetic society that change is possible, including arguments with a moral element such as slavery.

We probably all appreciate that "reinventing the wheel" isn't a great idea; but there are forces in modern life which make us do it anyway.[35] In workplaces or institutions, we are all at the mercy of the great game of corporate ladder climbing. If we are promoted to a new post, we will naturally want to make our mark. Especially if this new role involves some element of external security, we will probably initiate all sorts of extra programmes and implement extra systems to prove to our superiors that we really do know what we are talking about, and that we are well worth our salary. However, reinventing the wheel may be just the thing we need to do. If no-one had ever re-thought the design of a wheel, no bike would have spokes, and most would still be made of wood.

Change therefore happens when someone has an appetite for it, not necessarily when such change is needed or agreed on. We like to think that human ingenuity is expanding steadily and equally in all spheres of human understanding, but the reality is very different. Not only do we frequently reinvent the wheel in order to look dynamic and important, we can waste days of our working lives trying to redefine the wheel. The overarching message of these two chapters would be that change does not come about when the best argument 'wins'. Instead, change happens because somebody engaged with the peculiarities of why people and systems change in a more effective way than someone else.

Knowing all that you now know about failure and resistance to change, you will be better equipped to engage the right people with the right ideas in order to push your argument forward, and to recognise when resistance to change is an excuse rather than a valid argument. Address fears of the future with a constructive message of hope. Encourage, cajole and incentivise some limited risk-taking behaviour, and build cultures where failure is tolerated within a robust system of feedback.

Chapter 4

But the economy will collapse

Some ideas are so widely accepted that any challenge to them seems utterly incomprehensible. The compromise is so settled, that fundamental reassessment seems futile, like King Canute trying to negotiate with the tides. Ideas of human origin from one generation become self-existent forces of nature to the next. They are fertile ground for the comfortable compromiser to lay down his roots of inertia and grow bumper crops of excuses to stop you in your tracks. Such ideas are based on many assumptions about the way societies and human beings behave and interact, but you can't challenge them because people feel to do so would be to challenge this 'common sense'.

Economics is one such area of human activity. It has become central to our understanding of the world and ourselves - and only comparatively recently. When we identify an unjust situation where humans or animals are being exploited, the most common argument raised to justify the continued existence of the activity is one of economic necessity. Loss of jobs, income, taxes, however you seek to package it, we fear economic losses more keenly than anything else, and turn a blind eye to manifest injustices for the sake of maintaining economic benefits. We struggle to conceive of alternatives to the way our economy is organised to the extent that we assume it must be self-existent.

Questioning the compromise of economic organisation is necessary, but incredibly difficult. As a discipline, it rests on assumptions and decision making short-cuts which the compromiser exploits to make his case for continuance of the status quo. The financial crisis which began with the American sub-prime mortgage market and the intricate financial product devel-

opment by investment banks and has lately undermined single
European currency has created a window for questioning the
established economic order. Understanding its excusers demands
a little basic education on this fundamental element of societal
organisation. In this chapter we'll briefly explore its roots, core
assumptions and its weaknesses as a principle for societal organisation, in order to better unsettle our comfortable compromiser.

'Economics' is not neutral

Economics is at heart a social science grounded in reality, not an
ethereal exploration of abstract notions. I have a mediocre
knowledge of the classics from my Northern Grammar school
upbringing, enough to drop the Greek word "oikonomia" into
the conversation as the root of the word economics, meaning
'management of the household'. It has to do with deeply practical
matters - how we spend our resources, how we plan for the
future, how we make sure what we do is sustainable. It's development has taken twists and turns involving debates between the
great minds of several centuries, but one fact should be stated at
the outset; it should not be seen as absolutely normative or
objective. We do not slavishly follow the 'objective truths' of
economics in quite the same way as we must follow the laws of
physics or chemistry. There may be areas of established thinking
which have proved helpful in managing and organising modern
societies, but their interpretation into policies is not automatic
and should always be open to question.

   In fact, it is our view of society which informs our view of
economics. At its most basic, we are capitalist or socialist. Either
markets control us, or we control the markets. Our recent history
has seen the latter paradigm eroded, and the former elevated to
dominance. There is little fresh ideology to challenge the
dominance of the market economy as the least worst way of
organising society, at least in the more developed world. In
European politics, genuine 'left wing' or socialist policies have

lost their mass appeal. Most parties clog up the centre, with a few deviations to the right or left here and there. The zeitgeist states that markets should be free, and entrepreneurs should be encouraged as a means of national salvation. Since this plays to people's selfish interests, such parties are electable. No alternatives really exist. The market economy and its growth is the fundamental organising principle for society, an essential means of measuring our progress and success. To propose interfering with it in a public debate, and to even consider restricting its growth in some way will be greeted with howls of derision. Our economy has become a proxy for our lives. This is why making excuses based on economic common sense is such a powerful argument.

Growth

Political careers live or die by growth figures. Consumer confidence, the housing market and remuneration levels are all linked to our general sense of confidence in the economy, measured by the national statisticians as Gross Domestic Product (GDP). If the number goes up, we assume this is good. If it goes down, things are getting worse. We assume all growth is good and all recession is bad. Recession is very obviously linked with job losses, devaluation of assets and cuts in public services. Growth is assumed to benefit all these areas. Is all growth economic, and is all additional economic activity counted in the stats beneficial to our welfare as a society?

If someone opposes your plan on the basis that it will affect 'growth' in some nebulous manner, you have an opportunity to push them for more debate and some specifics. Growth is assumed to be a general good in society, and although it might be hard to debate such issues in the mainstream media, there is a well developed body of very serious thought which has challenged our conception of growth and its adoption as the central principle by which all policies and actions are judged. Its a vital weapon in your armoury, and possibly vitally important to your continued existence.

Firstly, growth is only a good thing if the space you are growing into is infinite, and if the resources fuelling your growth are similarly self-replacing and perpetual. We are becoming more aware of the limits to our growth in purely physical terms, since we only have one planet to live on. The problem with the reliance on economic growth as a benchmark for understanding societal progress is that it is an insubstantial concept which depends on very real things and people. The world now has seven billion people in it, all needing clothes, food and shelter. There are not unlimited amounts of the basic materials of life on which we can rely. At a basic physics level, the dynamics of energy use and availability rely on a finite resource, fossil fuels which represent the sun's stored energy. These problems have not been relevant until now, because the relative sizes of the finite resources and the global population were enough for us to effectively consider the resources to be infinite. As we push up against the ecological limits of our ecosystem, we realise that there may be a limit to our human growth, at least as we currently understand it.

Secondly, the concept of growth that is protected as the central goal of society is poorly defined and measured. When we think of growth and recession, we think first of GDP, or gross domestic product. Like many troubling concepts, it has been used for purposes for which it was never intended. GDP was conceived in war time as a means of measuring in some overall way the gross output of a national economy. It is a tally of all economic activity in an economy. Every product sold, every service used and every profit made. When GDP goes up, we are happy. When it doesn't we are worried.

GDP maintains such a position of reverence because of an important and misconception, namely that increased GDP means that societal welfare has increased. One a superficial level this holds true, since more jobs mean more people able to satisfy their basic needs. However, GDP counts *everything* that involved some kind of economic transaction on the positive side of the tally, not just the good stuff. The Gulf of Mexico oil spill could conceivably end up being positive for American GDP, because it forced the expenditure of billions of dollars on clean up (once the negative effects on fishing and other affected livelihoods are taken into account). Catastrophic failures of infrastructure create more spending. Not only does GDP count as positive those things which negative affect our welfare, it fails to account for many things which actually improve it. Voluntary workers make an extraordinarily useful contribution to modern society, from child care and education to home care and voluntary charity work, yet none of them are included in the GDP calculation since they are not salaried. Secondly, ecosystem services are 'free' and hence not valued. By this I mean the basic processes on which life depends - the carbon cycle, most importantly - and the positive benefits of a diverse ecosystem in terms of clean air, water, and as a source of useful chemicals and compounds is not well captured and valued. The interplay of the two factors produces perverse results. Deforestation of the entire Amazon basin would create a short-term boost in GDP through sales of timber, but the long term effects from soil degradation, erosion and the lack of carbon-fixing would be disastrous.

Finally, growth is assumed to be good since it will positively affect everyone - automatically. The standard metaphor is that of various sized boats floating in a harbour - "the rising tide floats all ships". This assumption has also been challenged. Growth in a market economy is unequal since incomes are distributed unequally according to market principles, not need.

The 'Market'

In our society, an idea can become so widely accepted that to even think of challenging it risks ridicule. Free trade has risen to this lofty height. A key political narrative centres around the market, and how free of government intervention it should be, and the widespread belief in the good of the market is fertile ground for excuses for inaction. Generally, since Adam Smith, people have agreed that introducing markets in things has been a more efficient way to generate growth, jobs and the capital surplus that enables the investment in the things we need. Most people when pressed would accept capitalism as the least worst option available to us.

The attraction lies in the fact that we do not have to confront human selfishness to solve our problems. In fact we embrace it, as Jerffery Sachs explains:

"Markets are wonderful because they coordinate the actions of a vast number of suppliers and customers who can remain largely unknown to one another . No great ethics or acts of courage, or virtues of coordination are needed, only the decentralised self-interest of each business and each consumer" (Sachs, 2008).

A quick glance around the global economy will show that markets vary wildly in their controls and values. Gaining widespread cooperation around a global goal has proved elusive through reliance on markets. They clearly work in some fields - but the results are often perverse to the socially-minded global citizen. Markets have ensured the near global distribution of soft drinks to quench our thirst, even in the most remote areas of sub-Saharan Africa, without any need for subsidisation or construction of infrastructure. Yet the penetration of life-saving vaccines into the same areas has enjoyed nothing like the same success. Back to Sachs:

"Markets fail when the poorest of the poor cannot afford to take part in them or when private incentives don't operate properly to provide public goods, such as environmental protection or disease surveillance or scientific breakthroughs, which are predictably underfunded by market forces alone."[36]

The free trade mantra relies on Adam Smith's invisible hand; we don't exactly know how it coordinates self-interest into a system maximising everyone's benefit, but it does it through price, and supply and demand. However, it rests on assumptions, as we have seen. If your plan involves the intervention into the market, these assumptions provide a basis for challenging any attacks you may receive for being 'socialist', so they are well worth a little more explanation.

To recap, the assumption is that in a perfect market, supply and demand work to dynamically balance each other until an optimum price and level of supply is reached. This rests on certain conditions being in place. The most important is that of perfect information. It is assumed that all players in the market will make perfectly rational purchasing decision, based on perfect information. So as a consumer, you would never pay full price for shoddy goods. You are able, at zero cost, to research the entire market in a product and make the absolute best purchase. The second is that all products are the same - meaning there is no variation in quality, and you always get a reliable product. Third, the supply end is made up of many small firms, not a big monopoly. Consider the markets you form part of, say your weekly grocery shopping. Are all your purchasing decisions purely rational, are all goods the same and is the market free from monopolies?

So much for the amateur economics lesson. How does this apply in an advocacy situation?

The US healthcare debate has been one of the bitterest the current century has known. Fuelled in part by the deep political polarisation on show in the States, it has been something of a 'theatre of war' for compromisers and their excuses. A key thread of the wider political debate in the US revolves around the role and size of the state. The 'Tea Party' movement advocates decentralisation and a small state 'machine' in favour of free-er trade and market based solutions. The more left-leaning areas of American society see a continued and expanded role for state provided services, such as healthcare.

Faith in the free trade, market-based system to deliver lower costs is often misplaced. Key figures in the healthcare debate continued to assert that free markets were the way to deliver healthcare, mainly on the cost argument. They retain this belief even when it is pointed out to them that practically every country delivering a centralised healthcare system does it cheaper than the current US arrangement. In many markets like this, the consumer doesn't have the right information or background knowledge to make the right choice between two replacement hip joints, for example. In these cases, a panel of experts running a centralised procurement system is actually in a better position to make the right call, to bring the greatest benefit to largest number. The assumptions of perfect competition would say it would be best to let customers decide; but how could they genuinely decide whether one course of treatment would be better than another?

The general point is that the societal level benefits of free-trade - that we get optimum prices, levels of production and levels of quality much cheaper than we would otherwise - are observable mainly in smaller markets for consumer staples and other goods. A private firm in a free market will make clothing cheaper than a centralised government ever could. The difficulty comes when people read across benefits of discrete consumer markets into the services which have generally been thought to have been the preserve of the state. The experience of introducing privatisation in the UK has been mixed to say the least; but costs have spiralled in privatised industries including public transport, utilities and constructing and operating hospitals.

The major reason for this is marketing costs. When private actors are introduced, the market dynamics are such that good products will stall against inferior but adequate ones if their marketing is poor. Marketing medical procedures such as scans to healthy people doesn't benefit them; neither does marketing drugs by name when there are cheaper generic versions out there. The comedian David Mitchell made a similar point about marketing in the UK train network. As the nationalised rail systems was privatised, private firms were formed to run key 'franchises' auctioned by the government. These companies market as if they are national companies competing against each other, whereas in reality they are discrete regional monopolies. They invest in better food, seats with airline style entertainment screens and other bells and whistles, supposedly in the effort to differentiate themselves from the competition. But the marketing makes no difference to the average user, and he is not making his decision based on what company has the best coffee, but where he needs to go. I'm a regular user of one of the busiest commuter train lines outside of London. I have had better coffee on other trains, but if I need to get to London, I have no option but to use this train company. I wont suddenly decide to go to Aberdeen instead because the cappuccino is better. The marketing cost is arguably wasted.

Excused by taxes and jobs

We now know that power of appeals to the very general principles of growth and free markets. Our next genus of economic excuses is tax and employment. Various controversial and damaging activities have been sustained because of the benefits of taxable income to wider society. In my lifetime, tobacco products have been proven to have serious health impacts, and yet the industry continues, mainly as a source of tax income. Similarly, the banking crisis of 2008 can be viewed as the result of a Faustian pact between New Labour and the financial services industry. An era of deregulation allowed a boom in complex debt instruments, with scant heed for capital adequacy limits sparked a booming services industry, the tax revenues from which helped to fund Labour's spending programmes.

But taxes have long provided excuses for allowing and damaging behaviours. Looking back at a case study of social change *par excellence*, Prohibition, we see how the need for tax revenue contributed to the repeal of the ban on alcohol sales.

The the stock market crash of October 1929 triggered the Great Depression. Demand for alcohol remained as steady as ever, but disposable incomes fell dramatically. However, the real boon to the campaign for repeal of Prohibition was a much wider economic argument. By making the industry illegal, the US Government had robbed itself of a vital and lucrative source of tax revenues, ones which were sorely missed as the administrators sought to fund the interventionists policies summed in the New Deal. Many saw the successful, legal industry in the UK (for example) and wondered if a similar regimen applied to the states wouldn't provide enough revenue to almost eradicate even the need for income taxes!

Resolving such issues is not easy, as the benefits of increased spending on public services were clear to the UK.

An important line of attack from this economic argument is to take a wider view of the full costs and benefits of the activity. Tobacco retail brings in tax revenue which funds the NHS; but how much extra money does the NHS spend treating entirely avoidable incidences of heart disease, cancer and respiratory conditions? The financial services industry brought in both tax revenue and a source of economic growth with kept the treasury healthy for a time; but in 2008 a bailout package for troubled banks such as Northern Rock and Lloyds TSB would trigger drastic spending cuts and an age of austerity, sparking increased unemployment and reduced access to vital services. Was it worth it?

Employment

Jobs are the sacred cow of modern discourse. Job losses are headline news. Unemployment rates will likely have a considerable impact on the fortunes of democratically elected governments. Things which create more jobs are good, always, without question.

Leaving aside the debate as to whether all jobs are beneficial to the person employed or to society in general, one of the easiest ways to engage the fear response is to link your plan to the threat of job losses. The writer Charles Handy reminds us of the relative freshness of our obsession with employment and jobs, at least as labels. Being known and identified primarily as an employee is a phenomena only about 100 years old.

> "If work were defined as activity, some of which is paid for, then everyone is a worker, for nearly all of their natural life. If everyone were treated as self employed during their active years then by law and logic they could not be unemployed. They might be poor but that can be put right. The words 'retirement' and 'unemployment' used only as a contrast to 'employment' would cease to be useful."[37]

There is a clear link here to the weakness of GDP as an indicator of welfare, since we have a prejudice towards to benefit of salaried jobs over voluntary or unpaid positions. All jobs which are paid are assumed to be 'good' since they lead to the payment of taxes and the creation of consumer spending, oiling the wheels of our creaking economic machine. Imagine a friend who has given up work to look after children. This is about the most demanding and full-time job that exists. Contrast this 'job' to something economically productive but ethically questionable, like equity release. Without wishing to condemn an entire industry, there are certainly some unscrupulous financial advisors who hoodwink their clients into paying exorbitantly high fees for their remortgaging. Which was more beneficial to society? Measured in terms of GDP, the con-man wins, hands down. Their is no way of attaching a tangible value to the production of well-balanced young men and women through the dedication of 18 years of parenting. Economically, we'd all be better off outsourcing childcare to specialists while we go out and earn money and pay taxes. This is the kind of perverse logic that over reliance on economics as an organising principle leads us into.

From citizens to consumers

Allied to our new understanding of the dominance of the market we must explore not just the feted position of consumers in society, but they way in which civic responsibility has been diluted down into a duty to spend rather than save. It is also a source of many societal problems, since being a consumer is to act to satisfy very short-term needs, often sending resources away from the long-term problems which need solutions. Understanding the prevalence of consumerism not just as a lifestyle choice but as our primary identity involves thinking about how we see ourselves.

> "People who devote a disproportionate share of their time to consumption do so not simply because of advertising indoctrination or never-ending panics, but because (aside from trying to gratify pleasures) in society as it is, the role of the consumer is the *most feasible arena in which to pursue freedom and dignity (emphasis added)*. In a mass consumer culture, such pursuit is displaced effectively from the ethical and political and economic arena into one of consumption, due to a series of active resolutions of an inherent tension between thought and action" (De Luca)

To be a consumer is to express your personal freedom and choice in the last sphere available to you. We can therefore excuse any tinkering with the market which might increase justice, fairness or welfare for the weakest on the world by stating that consumers should be the answer, and if we meddle with their preferences we undermine their very liberty. We want the ability to make choices, since it makes us feel free. But these choices are often divorced from ethical and political reality. What shampoo I choose may reflect the kind of person I would like to be, or what coffee I choose may send signals to the people I want to like me that I'm "one of them". The choices offer rewards, but they do not increase welfare in society. There is little real difference between the vast array of shampoos and coffees available to you and I. But the freedom we get from the illusion of choice is what is attractive.

Incentivising desirable behaviours is one economic route to attaining your goals, exploiting this avenue for expressing our freedom- whether it be through providing additional benefits for 'right' spending decisions or taxing 'wrong' ones. Not all incentives are created equal, however. Global supermarkets and retailers have been involved efforts to cut the use of disposable plastic bags, which often end up in landfill.[38] The relative success of two schemes gives an interesting perspective. Retailer A had a well established rewards point system; customers using their own bags would be credited with rewards points with the equivalent value of a few pence. Using the store's disposable plastic bags carried no penalty. Retailer B made a blanket decision not to give out free plastic bags; customers were then charged a few pence for every new plastic bag they had to use on a each shopping trip. Retailer B was hugely successful in reducing plastic bag use. Retailer A was not. Both systems involved the customer making the extra effort to remember some plastic bags. This involves a mental calculation - is it worth my effort? Customers, it seems, value an penny saved more than a penny earned. We will take steps to avoid incremental additional costs, but we won't take the same steps to gain an incremental advantage.

The faith placed in consumers to make the 'right choices' and hence shift the responsibility for deciding between options rests on a key assumption - that the consumers are a rational bunch who will appraise all the facts available to them and make a good choice. So instead of banning products made with, for example, bonded labour, we should provide information on the packaging detailing the specifics of the supply chain. Consumers, made aware of this reality will choose the 'better' option. Except which of us is truly rational in any area of our lives, let alone consumption, the cornerstone not just of modern society but modern identity? Why do we maintain consumption patterns in the face of changing circumstances, racking up debt or becoming addicted? Conversely, why do we abandon established consumption patterns in the light of the same changing circumstances, indulging in 'splurges' and 'binges'?

Knowing your customers is a little bit like trying to catch a bubble. Once you get close, the whole understanding of their motivations collapses. The differences between the energy providers in the UK is marginal, yet we all seem to shift suppliers on the basis of personal visits, or faddish offers. Consumers are also not one homogenous group, a fact which the large retailers know and exploit. They are endlessly subdivided into separate groups, with different motivations, worries, attitudes to price and conceptions of value. An appeal to the market is on many ways an appeal to the rationality of consumers. Essentially we cannot be trusted to make the 'right' choice for society, since the level of personal debt shows that we frequently make the wrong choices for ourselves. We consumers are capricious and fickle.

Believing that people will make the 'right' choices with their own money and hence allocate resources to the 'right' technologies and products, thus saving the world, is flawed in another major way. For the argument to work, a consumer must have limited resources. He must have a very definite amount of spare money to spend, in order for him to make the basic calculations of welfare that the assumption of consumer rationality depends on. With the advent of mass credit we stopped being limited to what resources we have, and became only limited by the amount of debt someone was willing to risk us having. People now satisfy not just their needs with what money they have, but the majority of their wants and needs through their earnings and expected earnings, brought forward into the future by consumer credit.

Consumers therefore allocate resources to short-term gain, not long-term welfare. They effectively reallocate future resources to the present, encouraged by advertising to not wait to own later what they could get on credit now. If we trust in the market economy to allocate resources to things that matter, we must account for the effect of consumer credit on the decisions consumers make.

Changing views on markets

The emergence and development of the environmental debate has seen a shift from the dominance of market thinking to more detailed, intricate views. It used to be fairly simple, as an industrialist in the early 20th century. Natural resources were there for you to acquire, consume and dispose of as you wished, according to your own appetite and financial constraints. The market transferred these resources around. Disputes which arose between parties were handled by adversarial disputes in court, settled by financial penalty. Polluters paid fines or damages. Behind this all was as assumption that the environment was generally very resilient to human activity, and could pretty much be trusted to recover from the impacts of environmental damage.

Views have changed. The value to human society of whole ecosystems, not just in terms of their values as commodities such as timber, is now being Better understood. Perhaps through the influence of Darwin and increasing understanding of people as part of a continuum of development of the environment, we now understand that the full 'value' of a forest, for example is not just represented in the value of the wood that can be sold to furniture companies. The local community gets the benefit of clean water and benefits from stable soil and lack of erosion from the root networks. Local livelihoods are supported by the flora and fauna. Global society as a whole gets the benefit from the process of photosynthesis, with the forests acting as carbon sinks. Importantly, these systems do not degenerate, but naturally regenerate and develop complexity if left to their own devices or actively and intelligently managed. But these values are not priced because they are not 'owned' by some specific party. So the market has traditionally undervalued natural resources and their cumulative benefits. We now understand this, and regulation in the West has changed to reflect this understanding, to a significant degree.

The existence of purely competitive markets isn't enough to protect valuable ecosystems, since the market fails as all prices are not accurate. This is a good means to challenge someone's assertion of 'market dominance' or blind faith in such transactions. Are you really sure that everything is priced in correctly?[39]

What works at the small scale . . .

A final concept to explore in the dominance of economies and markets in the public consciousness is the difference between micro-economics and macro-economics. By this I mean small scale markets with discrete boundaries, which are relatively easy to understand, and the big, globalised markets which are complex and difficult. An excellent example is the debate around developing country debt. The concept of forgiving debt is a difficult one for modern audiences to grasp, since we make the mistake of translating our private experiences of consumer credit onto the global scheme and make assumptions about what is fair and right. In the developed world, we have seen the poisonous effects of an over-reliance on cheap credit in recent years - from sub-prime loans to credit cards, to debt consolidation loans where the loanee was encouraged to use the left over capital from the debt you couldn't afford for a holiday[40.] The very idea of 'forgiving' debt strikes against our sense of 'fair play', let alone our economy.

Our social contract is based on the mutual exchange of rights and responsibilities. Debt is an example of private exchange of such things - I get the money which you have lots of and don't need to do what useful activity I have an idea to do, and you get paid back in instalments, while retaining the legal right to pursue me for the full sum should I default, usually secured against some asset. If I've loaned you money, then you owe it to me, no matter what. If debtors were to be forgiven their debts, then where is the incentive to work hard, be frugal, do the right thing and repay ones debts? If debtors were let off their responsibilities, then lenders would just stop lending. This would have a drastic effect on the economy - as entrepreneurs would lose access to a vital source of start-up capital, and we as a society would lose a means of financing large public works such as transport or health infrastructure. Cancelling debt with no repercussions seems to encourage sloth and profligacy, undermining the very basis of the global economy. Most people are a slave to their mortgage in this country, working boring jobs for long hours to keep up repayments. If I have to sacrifice to pay my debts, then why should I support the cancellation of foreign loans to developing countries, many of which are poorly run and corrupt? So goes the argument.

But this is a misconception, based on one key error - *the translation of micro-economic concepts to macro-economic situations*. It is risky to translate private experience into public policy; it may win you votes, resonating with members of the public, but it will often blind your eyes to the actual nature of problem, and cut you off from potential solutions. In private, being out of debt may be a worthy goal. One can imagine the outcry from the investment community if a company eschewed the opportunity to issues bonds in the market, in the interest of being debt free. For companies and governments, *not* carrying debt is inconceivable; things are just different at bigger scales (even respected news sites get mixed up between the deficit and debt, so you're not alone).

This problem of scale is another aspect of the micro-macro trap. How can we conceive of $1trillion? We think of debts in terms of our daily interactions - the size of our credit card repayment versus our monthly income, or the size of our mortgage against our other liabilities. Everything seems ridiculously big when reported in the evening news, or when we see the ticker running round Time Square totalling up the American National Debt. But our sense of scale is skewed if we rely on personal understanding of number to try and understand national economies. $1trillion might be a perfectly reasonable sum of money, when looked at in the right context.

To return to developing country debt, there in fact existed in the 1990's a strong common interest in providing a degree of voluntary debt relief (by voluntary we mean that provided by national financial institutions and commercial lenders by means of mutual agreement, rather than by legislation). The debtor country is stuck. It cannot grow fast enough to ever hope to repay its spiralling debt. The country cannot make its repayments, so it takes out even more loans to cover them. At this stage there is no direct benefit to the country in terms of capital investment, since it all goes on servicing existing debt, further eroding its ability to grow and repay the loan.

The providers of the loans could insist on their contractual rights, bankrupting an entire country, but this would gain them nothing in the long run. Rather, it is in their interest to either scale down the repayment obligations, or postpone them, creating an opportunity for continued repayment, albeit at a reduced level.[41]

The financial institutions are not really concerned with the repayment of the debt, as much as they are with your ability to continue to make interest payments. In debt relief, the government of the developing country is still held accountable for a proportion of its debts, but has its cash-flow problem eased in a manner which should stimulate its economy rather than crippling it (all this assumes sound fiscal policy and strong government, two quite big assumption to make). This creates an opportunity for interest payments to continue, and an economy to grow; a win-win.

On the macro scale, debt relief allows for a continuance of the mutual exchange of rights and responsibilities. Rather than undermining the economy, it allows for a party's continued useful participation in it. Economic arguments often take this course, and politicians are particularly fond of making folksy appeals to our private experiences of economic situations to argue against macro-economic interventions. It is your job to point out when people are making this link, based in fact on a false premise - that what holds true for private transactions in the economy holds true for relationships on a global economic scale. As the debt relief situation shows, the truth is often more complicated and more interesting.

The economy and the end of slavery

Having now explored the prevalence of economics and market dominance in our thinking, it is easy to wonder whether any significant change could ever come about if it looked to undermine the basis of an economy. Historically, one event above all others gives us a glimmer of hope. The slave trade was the lifeblood of the world economy, yet it was abolished in the space of a relatively short space of time. How did this happen? In answering this question, we encounter some fascinating developments in economic thinking, useful for our own efforts to effect change and combat the compromisers.

As we have seen, we all interact with money, and in our consumer driven society we fear material poverty more than anything. Wealth flowed from interests in the slave trade; of this there was no doubt. Slavery brought lives of ease and luxury, even in the 17th and 18th centuries. Importantly, slavery was not seen as a substitution for expensive labour; these ideas were yet to be adequately formulated, and we would have to wait for Karl Marx and our friend Adam Smith to fully elucidate them. Rather, slavers thought that basic labour was impossible without compulsion; it just wasn't conceivable that anyone would perform demanding physical labour without being 'chained and whipped'.

Much of this was down to a 'prevailing view of government control'. People were not to be trusted in their acts and decisions, and self-interest was harmful to the community. It was not until the aforementioned Adam Smith's Wealth of Nations in 1764 and the widespread understanding of the 'invisible hand' of the market that people began to understand that a harmony of self-interest coordinated through the market could in fact bring benefits to society at large. Free market economics was in its infancy. State based command and control models were prevalent in all the major nations' economies. The introduction of the notion of market based incentives was crucial in assuaging fears of global economic collapse should the slave trade be ended. It filled an intellectual void which was the source of much fear among the wealthy and influential.

Into this debate stepped Adam Smith himself, elucidating a fascinating insight into the un-desirability of slavery in a modern state. He focussed on the lack of incentives available to the 'slaves', where they had no reason to work harder or smarter. This undermined the world as he saw it, disallowing the sponta-neous coordination wrought by market forces through the integration of various actors' self interests.

Where was the incentive to the slave to work harder, or

smarter, to improve the process within which he was involved? A slave works only to assure his only continued, relatively hopeless, existence. Any additional value from his work must be wrought by compulsion, physical and emotional threats, all of which destroy the worker's capacity in the longer term. Additionally, the slave incurs costs for his master; the freeman must pay for his own physical upkeep. As Smith put it, "The work done by freemen comes cheaper in the end that that performed by slaves".

Abolitionists were given an intellectual and logical basis on which to challenge the view that slavery was essential to maintaining Britain's economic dominance. By replacing slaves with free-men, they could cut costs and see dynamic improvements in their production processes. In reality slaves effectively subsidised their plantations with free labour. When forced to pay wages, this subsidy would lost in the short term. But in the longer term, the incentives shift back onto the Plantation owner, not jilted from their steady state of compromise, with clear incentives to invest in improved processes being offered through mechanisation etc. Certainly this vastly over-simplifies the history of abolition, but it exemplifies the way in which methods of economic organisation can be challenged and changed in a way which increases overall freedom and general welfare.

And relax ...

That signals the end of our whistle-stop tour of the concept of economics. There's been a lot of detail and a lot of examples, and no doubt more than a few supplemental questions in your mind. Emerging from the mass of information, certain patterns begin to emerge, like the recurring melodic motifs in a musical piece. The more we think about the subject, we see that it does not exist apart from society, but is a product of it. It is informed by values and preferences. When we see it for what it really is, intervention in the market is not such an abhorrent idea, since it is meant to serve us, not the other way round. When our principles of economic organisation begin to produce results which undermine societal well-being, we can not only challenge them - we can change them.

The important point is not to be too weighed down if the 'economics' appear to be against you. Often, people are actually making simple points about affordability rather than economic suitability, relying on the widespread acceptance of centrist economic philosophy to 'excuse' their compromise with the ill-effects of the systems they are involved in. Plenty of policies are pursued at the current time in the apparent face of economic logic. And economics itself is a divided discipline. If slavery could be overturned and the economy could survive, and in fact see Britain grow into a powerful industrial nation, then anything is possible. A growing economy can no longer be relied upon as proxy indicator of societal welfare, for all the reasons outlined above, and the complicating factor of inequality. There is a desperate need for robust intellectual research in this field, to come up with a credible economic philosophy which allows for development (not growth *per se*) within the bounds of social and environmental limits. It is not a valid excuse to say that righting a social and environmental wrong will undermine the economy or economic growth.

However, this chapter has discussed the prevalence of economic assumptions from a very general standpoint. The concepts may still seem irrelevant to the compromisers you encounter on a daily basis. However, we've laid the foundations for the next chapter, where we explore the more day to day application of economic excuses by the comfortable compromiser.

Chapter 5

But We Can't Afford It

Affordability, or rather the lack of it, seems to prime concern of those in charge of a department, project, organisation or even family. No-one wants to run things into the ground, overspending on inefficient projects, endangering their own security. This excuse is especially universal and of use to the comfortable compromiser because it rarely engages with the morality of a suggested action and has more to do with the means of achieving it. We have limited resources to commit to various actions, and so we can only fund a certain range of them. If your suggestion does not fit into the established budget, then it won't be affordable, either as an *addition* to funding existing activities, or *instead* of them. Financial affordability and funding arguments often become intense debates, where different programmes stand-off against each other, each grabbing frantically to protect their piece of the pie, or grab someone else's. The compromiser can step back, and continue feathering his own nest while you and someone else equally worthy scrap among yourselves for the few morsels which fall from the budgetary table.

However, we also hate saying 'no' to people. As social beings, we do not wish to be identified as the one who stops things happening, refusing to sanction a course of action. It is often easier to hide from the intense moral debate over an action by making it more 'concrete' and denying an argument for change on the grounds of affordability. Affordability and budgets are peculiar features of human organisations which have grown out of our evolutionary ability to perform inventories of our assets and capabilities, conceive of our various options and decide what resources to put towards which options in order to meet our goals. This has evolved alongside our development of a monetary system of exchange, in which our assets and capabilities are valued in a tangible way. Our choices have become defined as their expression in monetary form - a matter of whether we have enough money to afford them at the moment. Unfortunately, good ideas which challenge an already balanced budget get sidelined.

Again, this area is very fertile ground for the comfortable compromiser because it is a human idea which is accepted as self-existent common sense. We deal with money and our own personal budgets on a daily basis. Our ideas about money feel like things we 'just know' to be true. Before we can understand the affordability excuse, we need to reassess our conceptions of money. On the face of it, affordability and choices between different actions create some difficult contrasts. Why is it that we can usually find the money for bank bailouts, but the same money cannot be found to fund the health service? Is life really a matter of such choices? In answering this question and dealing with the affordability argument, we need to understand a little more about how finance works, and what we really mean by affordability.

What is money?

Our memories are very short. It's only comparatively recently that money as a system of exchange has come to dominate our lives. Historically, we have relied on a system of bartering and swapping to exchange at fair value. Commodity money was then used as a means of unitising these transactions, so that things with different values which couldn't be easily divided could still be exchanged. For example, it was impossible for me to swap you half of my cow for a sheep of the same value. This commodity money at least had some link to a real value, and persisted in some forms such as the gold standard. It was a kind of "IOU", a promise to pay the bearer an identified amount of the physical commodity to which it was linked.

The next stage in the evolution of money comes in the development of 'fiat' money, that which is not directly linked to any actual commodity or physical asset. In this system, value is created through faith and trust, as much through the perceived value of what the money represents.

A country's money supply can be divided into three main forms. Firstly, there are the notes and coins in physical circulation, and all the 'cash' in everyday bank accounts and short-term deposits. This category covers any money that can be used to make a payment quickly. The second category includes all the money described above, plus that which is included in time-limited savings and some investments - in short, anything which can be easily converted into cash. Finally, we have the final, broadest definition which includes the rest of our total savings, money held in institutional investments and other large, relatively less liquid investments.

A government can affect the money supply, since it is 'fiat' money, and doesn't have to be linked to an actual asset[42]. When most people think of such interventions, we think of printing more bank notes, probably conjuring up mental images of run away hyperinflation such as that experienced in the Weimar republic in the 1920's with German workers taking home a day's pay in a wheelbarrow of notes. But as we have seen, the physical notes are only a small part of the overall system. When governments resort to 'printing money' they perform an action know as "Quantitative Easing". This involves buying up government issued fixed income gilts on the on bond market. They 'create' the money, and transfer it to the people selling the gilt. This is a huge oversimplification, but the essential message is that money as we experience it at a personal or organisational level is a very different beast when considered at a national economy level.

'My money' and 'our money'

A recurrent theme of this book is the difference between discrete personal situations and more general, society level situations, and the lack of suitability of transferring our understanding of concepts at a personal level into the public sphere. When we become involved in an affordability debate, we in fact restrict ourselves to a method of decision making which relies on cost-benefit analysis. Costs at a personal level are much more certain that at a corporate level. I may know for certain how much my car will cost to insure and tax this year, and know within a certain range of prices what it may cost to run depending on a number of defined variables such as petrol prices. The trade off for me is clear; I know the costs of the car versus the costs of the bus for certain trips, and I make the decision which gives me the best utility at the best price. However, when thinking about the costs to society of the air emissions produced by the cumulative effect of an entire nation's vehicle use, we must somehow aggregate all of our preferences and pricing into one model. This is, needless to say, somewhat problematic.

Approaches which use cost-benefit analysis must draw on techniques which extract our collective preferences for different kinds of actions and collate them into one data set. The method leans heavily on the concept of 'revealed preferences' - inferring values from the choices people make based on their activity within a market. The number of people using public transport over private cars at different prices, for example, would reveal our preference for cleaner air over the utility of private transport. There are many problems with aggregating cost data in this way. Market values are affected by regulations, taxes and the existence of monopolies or cartels. Changes in one market may affect another, with unforeseen effects. Finally, the environmental 'good' - clean air in this case - is simply not traded and not prices, so it cannot be accurately included in the model. At a systemic level, cost-benefit analysis is loaded with such assumptions, all of which will undermine the reliability of the resulting affordability equation.

Assuming that the 'revealed' prices in the model actually reflect the genuinely held beliefs and preferences of the population you are sampling, more difficulty is encountered when people transfer these preferences into different scenarios. What you choose when presented with a range of choices is one thing; your preference for that action may not hold true if it were forced upon you. Most importantly, your private choice may reflect the fact that you simply do not know what is 'best' or 'more economic' for you. Privately, you may be opposed to Britain being in the European Union, while your workplace relies heavily on exports to Europe for its economic viability. You might not understand this, and see the personal costs of conforming to EU standards in the workplace as outweighing any benefit. However, without the wider benefit of the EU, you would not have a job in which to complain. Your economic preference has very limited viability. Hence the cost benefit-analysis is fraught with difficulties and assumptions, all of which can be cleverly used to manipulate our understanding within a simplistic veil of crude logic.

Slaves to the budget

The collective term for our preferences for spending our accrued and future resources is our budget. Deriving from the French word for purse, it embodies our plans for spending and saving. Budgets are hard enough for us to engage with when we are dealing with our personal finances, but take on an entirely new dimension of stress and difficulty when we are dealing with a large organisation, operating multiple programmes. At an organisational level, debates about the budget can take up large amounts of scarce time. Understanding how people make decisions about budgets and how they are characterised helps us to see why many feel they cannot afford to do new things, or why someone who is comfortable in the current compromise might use budgetary concerns as an excuse for inaction.

Theories of budgeting as relates to local government in the UK trace a development of thought from competition and rational allocation to incrementalism. That is a very uninspiring sentence, and it probably didn't catch your attention. What do I mean by this important statement?

The traditional view of deciding on a budget is to see it as a a process of bidding from competing departments. In the absence of any central data relating to the details of these bids with which to evaluate their merits, resources are divided up on an equitable basis. Extra money is divided up equally between the departments, and any cuts are imposed equally. In this model, the focus is on the future. The basic activities, the existing behaviours which had budget headroom were treated as self-existence and un-challengeable. Those programmes which already had funding are much harder to change, as most debate focuses on the allocation of surpluses or sharing cuts. Rarely does a financial controller have all the detail he needs to decide which programmes should stay and which should go, since every 'bidder' for scarce capital has an incentive to portray his department as vital, since their job depends on continued funding.

The social scientist Lindbolm suggested an alternative view to this competition for resources, arguing that budgeting was in fact a more incremental process. Budget makers do not have a mental conception of the 'entire pie' which they then divide up, but rather focus their efforts on making decisions at the margin. Rather than trying to come up with a full, detailed understanding of everything they do, they focus their time and energy on those decisions where they will be most relevant. The base of spending is assumed, and the 'fight' is restricted to a few incremental changes in the pre-existing budget.[43] This is sensible to a degree, since policy makers and those who decide budgets may not have choice over certain elements of the activities they will fund. They may be obligated by law to provide certain services, such as fire-fighting and education[44.] Decision makers exist inside the constraints of their activities, and so it makes sense to devote most of your time to those areas where your opinions and deliberations will actually matter and add value.

Such an approach creates the room for us to become slaves to the existing budget, missing potential new opportunities to cut waste and invest in better ways of doing things. If we can't afford to do something since there is no room in the existing budget, it may be that the existing budget is not being actively questioned. This incrementalism is not unrelated to the policy goals of an organisation, however. Lindbolm goes on to argue that the incremental analysis of budgets comes from the incremental politics into which it fits so nicely. Making large scale changes or re-evaluations might be the best way to go, but may be constrained by what is possible within the internal politics of the organisation. Such step-by-step approaches cannot react quick enough to a fast changing world. However, the degree to which an organisation is insulated against that change varies. Some public sector organisations may be especially change-insulated, especially if none of their stakeholders are making calls for change.

When budgets are allocated on an annual basis, spending patterns are influenced by the timing of the process. Most departments are asked to submit estimates for their activities for the next year, which will then be scrutinised by some central committee for accuracy, before a series of trading and bargaining between departments results in the setting of the budget. This process is reactionary, since it assumes that what you spent last year is roughly what you will need this year. It also encourages departments to spend money even when they don't really have to. The size of your budget is also a source of prestige within some organisations, and so there is an incentive to preserve what you already have, in order to look good in front of your colleagues, or vastly superior at the industry conference.

This results in a very lumpy spending pattern in most departments. Once budgets are granted there may be an initial rush of enthusiasm and a glut of spending, followed by a sobering sense of caution, as we don't want to spend everything right away. Projects will be then deferred or ignored. Towards the end of year, when estimates are being demanded, we may have all kinds of surpluses which we do not want to report to the financial controller, since we don't want them taken away. So we authorise a mad rush of work just before the end of the financial year. I suspect this process is behind the unusual amount of road works evident in February and March in the UK.

Such spending rarely delivers much benefit. In the town in which I grew up, I tracked the growth in miles of useless cycle lanes, ones set up where the road was already very wide, only to disappear on the junctions where you actually needed them. New road markings and paint sprang up about the same time each year. I have no conclusive proof that this was due to 'lumpy' and panic spending. But the budgetary process which creates the pressure to 'spend to protect' one's budget, not to deliver services which actually help people, could easily create miles of useless bicycle lane. Therefore, engaging with budget makers must be done within the appropriate timeframe, when there are resources available and when officials are in the frame of mind to spend money.

If we accept that budgeting is a mixture of rationality and incremental, marginal decision making, we can move on to the second question. That is - from what angle are budgets considered? Are they demand-led, from 'the bottom up', or policy lead - from 'the top down'? Deciding which is the most prevalent will have implications for your strategy. If they are demand led, the financial decision maker will consider all bids for useful activity according to his goals and decide what he can afford to fund in the next year. If it is policy lead, they will be influenced by their political masters into developing a strategy in which they will determine the overall amount of resources available for various projects. Deciding which tactic is being relied on is key in engaging a comfortable compromiser and getting money released for your idea. It's no use creating awareness of greater demand if policy makers prefers other options. Equally, it's no use engaging policy makers when budgets are decided according to needs.

In times of of austerity, we are dominated by a top-down approach. Governments identify the total level of resources which they consider sustainable in the longer term. They then decide on what priorities deserve continued attention despite a fall in the overall level of committed resources, and have therefore identified where the axe will fall. Moving toward the top-down approach is often a response to financial pressure, as we can observe from the manner in which local authorities in the UK adapted to the growing complexity of the services they offered in the 1960's and 70's, adopting a more corporate approach to managing budgets. The people involved appreciated that incremental action fostered a sense of departmentalism in which budgets were developed in relation to specific function, often with duplication of service. For example, the provision of ambulances, police cars and council vehicles, all with their own vehicle repair yards and mechanics. Executive level oversight was recommended as a means of dealing with this problem, with managers tasked with greater integration and coordination of budgets, recognising that every action to cut or promote some areas would have effects on another area.

There is a very important distinction to be made here between public agencies whose resources depend on tax income and companies whose resources depend on the distribution of profits. If sales of a product suddenly increase, a company will pump extra resource into matching production with the demand, in order to maximise profits. A public organisation is much more static. Since it is more responsive to policy goals, it is less responsive to demand. In fact, too much demand for a service can be a problem for public officials. Entering into budgetary debate with public bodies therefore takes a much different character, and the strategy for engagement should be tinkered to suit.

Engaging with those who have the responsibility for deciding what gets funded and what doesn't involves a recognition of the difficulty of the job. Few people, apart from a perverse and thankfully rare collection of horrible individuals, take pleasure in continually saying 'no' to worthwhile causes. Budgets, especially government budgets, are generally premised on an annual allocation funds, and may be susceptible to sudden changes depending on the political climate. Here is another example of the mis-match of human timing and commitment with the necessary time needed for changes to be effective. Long-term budgets are desirable, but open to being undermined by a rapidly changing political and funding context. Taking a long-term decision may benefit everyone, but you may not get any thanks for it in the short term (see below).

Finally, the influence of self-perpetuating incrementalism in budgets creates a very difficult environment for any new ideas to be tested, simply because they have not been tried in anything like the same scale as existing practices.[45] This means there is far less data to be poured over for the new idea, and much less evidence linking it to the desired outcomes. This is a technical block to new ideas.

Since budgets are complex, those skilled in their construction and portrayal can perform numerical conjuring tricks to make problematic budget features 'disappear'. In this way, budgets can be maintained by reclassifying different expenditures in different ways on the balance sheet. The simplest method is to turn current spending into capital expenditure, for example, turning everyday repairs from current costs into capital spending. Sale and leaseback is yet another almost ubiquitous method. Financial professionals are thought of as being obsessively concerned with spreadsheets, but they are just as capable of creative ingenuity within their field as any professional within the 'creative media'. The point is that budgets and their terminology can be manipulated to suit your purposes, and so getting some expert opinions on budgets and accounting is a smart move if you wish to engage on a level playing field.

Feeling the pinch in smaller settings

We rarely feel like things are going well financially, both personally and corporately. Making a crude generalisation, your organisation will either be for profit or not. Again, the question of scale is very important in this context. The budgetary constraint is a much more powerful argument when dealing with the smaller organisation, which lives a somewhat hand to mouth existence, where the lines on the budget worry the entire board of trustees. On a bigger scale, the questions are different. A national treasury doesn't sit down and work out how much money it needs to fund all the programmes the country needs. Rather, politicians and civil servants work out how much tax revenue they can gather without alienating a majority of the electorate, and then distribute it accordingly (usually according to who shouts loudest). It becomes a distributive negotiation, with clear winners and losers. But things can always be amended, and budgets can be changed.

Most of the discussion above applies to well funded organisations with clear long-term financial security, not terms which could be applied to the average NGO or charity. If you work in these organisations, you may be living a more or less hand to mouth existence based on what you can extract from donors or government departments, in which case your budget will likely be a matter of deciding which of a list of equally worthy things you can 'afford' to do at the moment.

Non-profit organisations often find themselves not only slaves to the budget, but to specific donors. Often a group which is feeling the pinch will find itself 'in' with a large donor, so large that it is dependent on their continued patronage in order to guarantee. The non-profit then chooses what to do based on what funding it will likely get, rather than deciding what it wants to do then going out and finding funding. Those within in the sector refer to this process as 'mission drift'. Obviously, departments within profit-making companies can exist in a similar context, being dependent on central budgets which seem to be under endless review and cost cutting.

Opportunity Costs

The "we can't afford it" excuse is actually more nuanced. The money might not be available right now, but that does not usually mean that there is no money available. It means that the money is already spoken for - i.e. certain priorities have already been established and funds for the them have been earmarked, meaning that no additional money is available for your new project. This naturally leads into phase two of the 'we can't afford it' excuse - that starting doing what your asking for will necessarily mean stopping doing something else, usually something emotive. This is expressed in economics as an 'opportunity cost'. We have a finite source of capital and an infinite source of potential options for using that capital. By choosing one thing, we lose the opportunity to invest in the other.

However, the argument can be manipulated to work the other way. During Prohibition it was argued that consuming alcohol was in effect an opportunity cost to society. Drunks spent their hard earned cash on whiskey and beer, when they could spend it on food for their families, education or healthcare. Prohibition would, it was assumed, stop the possibility of wasting your money on liquor, and move this expenditure into more positive arenas.

Except prohibition would bring costs, too, namely in enforcing a restriction on supply when demand was booming. Each unit of supply prohibited uses tax revenues which cannot then be used for education, say, or defence. Increasing taxation to fill the gap will hit household incomes - the very things which were assumed to have been liberated by Prohibition itself. Seen from this angle, we can see how adding a global economic depression into the mix would create a pressure for allowing significant taxation of a booming industry such as alcohol.

So much for the costs of doing one thing instead of another; we may also have to ask ourselves a further question - "Can we afford NOT to do it?". Rather than thinking about the immediate costs of implementation of a new programme, what are the long-term costs we will incur if we continue in the current manner? For example, we may have questions about the best way to regulate the social problem of binge drinking in the UK, from minimum alcohol prices to restricting opening hours. But the short term costs must be weighed against the long-term negative impacts of generations with a destructive relationship with cheap alcohol. What are the costs from lost productivity in the work place? What are the costs of the ill-health, and the number of beds taken up with people with avoidable illness caused by lifestyle choice, while those who are the cruel victim of circumstance suffer?

Numbers are scary

So far we've talked about the budgetary numbers in abstract terms. In reality dealing with numbers will often be done in committees. The finance stage of the agenda is a bit like watching the prequels to the Star Wars Trilogy - you feel it necessary, yet it's time consuming, unpleasant, met with relief once over and it leaves you with a faint a nagging sense of discomfort that you have missed something huge and been wronged in someway. There is no agenda item met with more dread and loathing than the budget. We all just want it out of the way quickly, and then we can move on. Are we solvent? Yes. Great. Next item.

The reality of numbers is unpleasant to anyone who actually dares to care or have an opinion. However, we more often than not choose to bury our collective heads in the sand rather than deal with the reality. On a personal level, not all of us can deal with the reality of financing and budgeting. There are rewards if we do, though, in saving up for things, not being in debt and having enough money around to spend on the things we need. But it is a lot of hassle, and many people who get into debt do so because they can't face opening the bank statement, working out the hard facts of their financial situation, and deciding what they can't afford.

There are some peculiar dynamics observable in committees and boards when it comes to discussion budgets and proposed expenditure which should give us cause to reconsider the validity of budgetary decisions made against us. This was described in timeless fashion by C. Northcote Parkinson in his seminal satire of modern life 'Parkinson's Law - The pursuit of progress' which fleshed out an earlier article for The Economist first published in 1955. The law we are concerned with is "the law of triviality" which can be summarised as the following:

"The Law of Triviality... briefly stated, it means that the time spent on any item of the agenda will be in inverse proportion to the sum involved."

The bigger the proposed expenditure in a meeting, the smaller the amount of time devoted to it. Parkinson tells a fictional story of a committee which manages to approve the construction of a multi-million pound nuclear project in a few minutes. They spend much longer on deciding the colour and construction of a bike shed for the employees. They spend *even longer* deciding on a request for a tiny addition to the budget for the clerks' hot beverages.

Why is this? The nuclear plant is vast and complicated. Only one person at the table knows very much about nuclear power, and while he has some fears about the contractors, he fears his fellow board members will not understand, and he can't be bothered spending the next twenty minutes explaining the situation to them. The others, who may have doubts but know he is the expert, say nothing for fear of being made to look foolish. The item is passed with minimal discussion, because no-one knows enough about the project and is too afraid to say so. The next agenda item comes up, with everyone feeling a little bit troubled that they said nothing on the multi-million project. So you get a few more opinions thrown in on the appropriate construction of the bike shed. What material should you use? People round the table might have some better understanding of building materials, and so they have their moment in the sun, opining about the benefits of galvanised steel. Before you know it, half an hour has passed, as the members of the board take turns to demonstrate that they are knowledgeable and helpful. Finally, we move on to the request for extra money for tea bags, and all hell breaks loose - because everyone, everywhere has an opinion on how to make team, how to economise, how we could save money, how long the clerks' break should be in the first place. And so passes the rest of the meeting – a whole hour to decide the fate of £10, 3 minutes to decide on the investment of £10million.

Challenging the affordability excuse - innovative financing

Most proposals fail the affordability test because they approach it in a one-dimensional manner. You have an idea for a programme which needs a certain amount of money to get it off the ground. If all you offer are costs, then you are easier to reject. It's better to rethink your proposal in terms of what you will be bringing should your programme be successful, - quantifying the savings you might bring to your potential funder.

Social finance is one such field where innovation is bringing very different funding actors together to work for social benefit. To take one example, the issue of prisoner re-offending is causing difficulty in the UK currently. Detaining prisoners is costly, and an estimated 60% of prisoners on short sentences reoffend within a year of their release, seeing prison populations soar and costs increase. Intervening to reduce reoffending through a network of small measures in the third sector has been proven to be effective at reducing reoffending, and hence saving the authorities money, but there is a 'time-lag' between investing in the prevention systems and the ultimate cost saving to the government.

Into this gap steps the social impact bond. Money from private investors is invested in a bond structure which funds rehabilitation programmes. If the initiative reduces reoffending by an agreed percentage, then the Government has agreed to share with the investors a share of the cost savings.[46]

The Government cannot afford to fund the rehabilitation programmes, because the pay-back is too long term (and would likely benefit another administration), and so the situation looked to be at an impasse. The innovation detailed above flips the affordability argument on its head, and changes the questions being asked entirely. Instead of calling for a change in budget to fund your ideas, you are asking for permission to spend other people's money in order to deliver cost savings for the Government. You are, of course, asking them to shift their thinking on an issue, and experiment with an innovative finance model, but what has the Government got to lose? The investors took the risks, and the Government only has to share some of the benefits derived, ones which it couldn't afford in the first place. This is dealing with the argument at its most basic. If you can't win the affordability argument, seek ways to change it from a fight over limited resource into a sharing of benefits.

When can we afford it?

The cost and affordability excuse can run parallel with excuses based on timing. Since income is fluid, and to be understood with reference to what we have, what we've committed to spend and what we're sure we'll get in future, then affordability can change daily. The most common objection, which we'll explore in more detail in chapter 9, isn't simply that we can't afford it, but that we can't afford it *right now*. This is a very important distinction, especially for the person blocking your plan, since he looks like someone in favour but constrained by circumstance, powerless in a sea of shifting financial situations, empathetic to your plight, but ultimately unable to help at this moment.

Timing and affordability do not always seem to always work against each other, especially if you consider some great historical changes. If you talk with someone from mainland Europe about the NHS, it will seem odd to them that the UK could 'afford' to run a health service which is free at the point of use. Maybe your discussion will touch on the origins of the health service and indeed the whole engine of the modern welfare state constructed by the post-war Labour Government dealing with a devastated country.

There never was a more unlikely time to build a welfare state, from an economic point of view. Surely there were hundreds of other competing priorities? Surely there just wasn't the money available? The reality is that the population, galvanised and scarred by years of conflict, were ready to build a better society, reflected in the very fact that the Labour Party won the post-war general election, deposing on of the most popular leaders this country has seen in war time. The affordability argument slipped down the list of importance in the face of shared passion and desire to make a clean break with the politics and structures of the past. Ethics and notions of 'a better world' seemed more important than short term costs.

Moving into the modern day, the most significant challenge

we face is the under-cutting of the budgets of the very welfare state which was erected in the 1950's, thanks to a private sector financial crisis which needed a multi-billion pound financial rescue package. Necessity creates money. The British Treasury didn't have that money just lying about in gold deposits or foreign currency. It created the financial reality, augmenting the situation further by the 'money printing' of quantitative easing. When the crisis is big enough, we find the money.

Of course, I am not saying that we can always afford everything we want to do. The printing of money and the bailouts through creation of debt are the last resorts, since they undermine global confidence in a national economy, just as you would be rightly concerned to lend more money to someone who has already maxed out three credit cards and has remortgaged their flat twice (although you have to be careful not to read across lessons from your personal life to national economics!). Credit cards create money based on an assumption of future earnings, but most people do not pay them off, preferring to move the debt around and keep in manageable in order to maintain a certain lifestyle. The same can be said for national economies.

My point isn't to debunk sound fiscal and budgetary policy, which we clearly need, and we haven't even considered the vitally important elements of inflation, interest rates and currency valuation. The key thing to grasp is that at national and international level, we can be an awful lot more creative than at the personal level. We do have more options for financing available to us. If we make our case well enough, or what we do is considered vital enough, then we too can be considered 'too big to fail' and affordability in the short term will not be a part of the equation. Money will be found, moved or created.

The most difficult situation comes when we cannot afford something in the short term which will cost us more in the long term. When the benefits accrue instantaneously to the person making the decision, whether in increased productivity or in 'kudos' for the astute management, you are more likely to be able to persuade someone to act immediately. However, when the reverse is true, the affordability argument is extremely powerful. If the benefits are all deferred, and the costs all immediate, then it takes a very brave person to enact the policy.

Added to this difficulty is the short-termism of electoral and political cycles. In Vancouver, where I am currently writing, there is a considerable risk of a major earthquake happening at some point in the next 20-30 years. There are areas of land which are more susceptible to damage during an earthquake close to the surface due to their geology and soil formation. These more low lying areas of the city require some remedial work and reinforcement of foundations in order to make them able to survive such an earthquake. Any investment now would be far less than the future cost of rebuilding an entire area of a city. However, in the short term, the cost is large.

The person making the decision will be judged within the next two years on his record. If he raises taxes to fund the work, he will take all of blame for affecting people's incomes. If and when such action was taken, and then an earthquake were to happen, no-one would likely remember his noble sacrifice. Politicians and those with public office seemingly have no incentive to make such mature choices. Short term affordability seems to trump nearly all claims for long-term investment. Sadly, this feature of politics is not limited to North America.

A final reflection - the ethics of affordability

Affordability itself is is seen by some as inappropriate for use as the basis for making decisions. Some values that we hold as a society rest in tension with pure cost arguments. The cost of palliative care for terminal cancer patients is, on the face of it, a waste of money, but surely something most people in society consider a cost worth bearing. Where issues of human suffering are involved, even raising the issue of costs can seem crass.

Assigning monetary values to human life jars us, but policy makers feel the need to assign some value to a human existence in order to make sense of their decisions. Considering a human life 'worth' or 'not worth' saving leads to moral outrage, as typified in decisions not to provide cancer treatments with only limited evidence of success to National Health Service patients in the UK. However repugnant we find such a valuation, and however much we would oppose it in public, we do such analyses in private, and avoid talking about the issue. Rather than stating clearly that the treatment simply does not have enough benefit to justify the costs - I.e. It does not save enough lives - the opposition will be more subtle and make the argument by inference, suggesting that the data is uncertain, or that more research is needed.

Sometimes social norms and cost-benefit analysis can seem incompatible. Imagine a confrontation between a parks commissioner and a parent whose child was killed after suffering head injuries following the use of a diving board in a public pool[47]. The parents want all such diving boards removed, and ask "how many more children will have to die before you do the right thing?"

"Who could imagine, or would want, the commissioner to answer, 'actually I've got that right here, the answer is two. My analysts have established that two children would have to die each summer before our net psychological quality of life figures would tell us to take the boards down"[48].

There are 'subtle and abstract ways' in which such apparently cold-hearted thinking actually works to the benefit of everyone. It may look distasteful when considered on an individual case basis, but the reality of large budgets and competing priorities forces our hand.

Widen the discussion

Wiping the metaphorical sweat from our brows after our two chapters on money and economics, we find that budgeting and cost-benefit analysis are an expression of our decision to manage society along the capitalist model, since they exert control on the allocation of capital. They are often the 'least worst' way of making difficult decisions. The debates around affordability must be approached with an appreciation of scale and timing. Do we need to reallocate a fixed amount of money, or can we create more? Can we do it now, or do we have to wait? Budgets are expressions of future strategy. If the comfortable compromiser in your immediate field of view makes constant appeals to the lack of budget room for new projects, then the argument is not over. The budget is not written in stone. If room cannot be found in it to fund the best interventions, then the strategy is represents is flawed.

The affordability excuse is sometimes a bluff. In most committees there are few financial experts; most financial decisions get passed on to the recognised financial expert. If this person is the compromiser who has something to lose from an otherwise positive change, they may state in vague terms that they think it is unaffordable, appealing to you to trust their judgement of the figures. Sometimes they are gambling that you won't try and dig into the figures yourself. Sadly, there is sometimes no alternative but to roll up your sleeves and seek to really understand and engage with the budget before you. But at least now you know the human elements behind it, how it has been constructed and how you can begin to work with it to unseat the comfortable compromiser.

Chapter 6

But 'The system' won't let us

"Computer says no"

Three words to ruin your day, a fact of modern life revealed in all its glory by the creators of "Little Britain". As I again show my dependence on BBC Comedy for context and material, let me explain the typical encounter. Bureaucracies and administration are built on systems and structures. More than ever, these systems are automated and computerised. Managers seek consistent decision making, and an expanding number of decisions are 'delegated' to computerised or automated functions. These systems can get in the way of a sensible decision, often to your cost. This is encapsulated in the comedy character in question, who had two jobs in the series, as a travel agent and bank clerk. In both situations the comedy was formulaic. The customer has a query, things look hopeful, then the assistant bashes in the data into the machine. The assistant looks up from her screen and delivers the verdict. The computer says no.

The appeal to the dominance of an external system is a barrier to reasoned debate, classified by Feldman as an 'argument stopper', something we'll discuss in more detail in the next chapter). People trust their systems more than their own common sense, and retreat into their boundaries for comfort, refusing to discuss extenuating circumstances. But the 'systemic malaise' (to coin a phrase) goes much deeper in a age of increasing regulation and political correctness. Organisations can feel surrounded by interest groups and regulation; they fear the Equal Opportunities Commission, the Competition Commission, the Financial Services Authority and the Serious Fraud Office. They tremble before Human Rights, Employment Law and Environment

Agency, before they open the can of civil law worms that is tort and personal injury litigation. Surely someone, somewhere has a interest in stopping us doing what we are being asked to do?

Once again, we see a troubling facet of developed society which easily exploited by the comfortable compromiser, the second concept on which we over-rely, giving the compromiser a chance to halt progress and excuse damaging behaviour. The awareness of vast and intricate 'systems' set up to deal with the difficulties of coordinating time and resources can be played upon by those who benefit from their position within those same systems. We need some specialisation in society, and certainly we require specific and discrete areas of law and regulation to curb our more damaging behaviours. But it may be that we have become so reliant on structures and systems that we have failed to live up to our own individual responsibilities. How has this occurred?

The enemy is out there

We are supposed to be more free than ever. Yet why do so many of us feel so small, so powerless in the face of global and national political structures? We can feel impotent in our efforts to change anything, as someone else always seems to have the real power. Ignoring the issues of authority and power for a moment, we must deal with bureaucracy, complex administration and red tape. Engaging with a movement for change may mean engaging with an administrative process which will drain the life out of you.

Our negative experiences with poor administration lead us to avoid any prospect on engaging with them again, unless we absolutely have to. No doubt you have been exasperated as a long wait to be dealt with in a call centre results in a conversation in which you are mis-heard and mis-understood, then finally think you've got your message across, only to have the same letter come in a week later, as the issue hasn't been resolved. We feel aggrieved as our precious time has been wasted. Our lives are stressed and pressured, and we think twice before trying to change anything if it might involve an administrative battle.

The management writer Charles Handy identified the philosophical roots of our 'systemic malaise', observing that most of us feel at the mercy of forces beyond our control:

"Too many delegate their futures and their questions to some mysterious 'they'. 'They' will set the syllabus for life just as 'they' set the syllabus for our courses at school. 'They' know what is best, 'they' must know what they are doing. 'They' are in charge, leave it to them. The phrases and excuses are endless. One of the strange things about growing older is the gradual realisation that 'they' don't know, that the Treasury is not all wise, and that 'they' are on the whole just like you, muddling through, and not very interested in you, anyway."[49]

Opposition is sometimes more imagined than real. We have all kinds of fears of difficulties problems which we are sure must exist, since we have heard of other's negative experiences. In reality, we have not tested the waters ourselves, to take the actual temperature. We just assume that change will be opposed, since it will mean more work for someone. The system of political and economic control will get in the way.

To an extent, this syndrome is being eroded. Confidence in politicians in the UK has been seriously undermined by the recent expenses scandal - what little was left after decades of 'sleaze'. The continued economic crisis leads many to question whether the people in charge really do know what they are doing, even to the extent of setting up camp on Wall Street or outside St Paul's Cathedral. If the authorities are just like you, they may be more desperate for your help than you know. You may find a willing, resourced partner in one you previously supposed to be an enemy. They may be exhausted, and out of ideas, in which case they may be more open to your plan than you think.

The dominant systems

On that note of optimism, we can begin to explore some of the more mis-understood systems which dominate modern life. Our fear of these systemic forces often rests in misunderstanding and ignorance. There is often a 'gap' between public understanding of a system of regulation and the actual role, values and benefits of that system. Whilst we'll take some extended time to discuss four 'systems' which are misunderstood, the salient point is this; systems and structures such as these are human constructs, run by humans and subject to misunderstanding.

1. Health and Safety

The Health and Safety Executive has a pretty bad name in the UK, an inexhaustible source of stories for popular press columnists. The citizens of the UK recently celebrated their glorious monarchical tradition / Exacted an extra day's holiday from the 'system' (delete as appropriate) when two posh people got married in a big church. It was very nice. People had street parties. The proportion of lemon drizzle cake per square mile in the UK rose to the highest level since Tim Henman last tried very hard to get to a Wimbledon final.[50]

Some people were reportedly thwarted in their attempts to organise a convivial community gathering on the street, due to 'health and safety'. Rumours and scare stories abounded about anyone providing food having to gain clearance from the relevant authority, and wear a hair net, and have a letter from your mother given you permission to exceed your recommended daily allowance of trans-fats, etc. The HSE cried fowl, and produced a special edition of its 'myth-busting' section on its website. Portrayed as a misanthropic killjoy, as it often is, the HSA responded in the following fashion:

"There's nothing in health and safety law to prevent anyone from celebrating the Royal Wedding - in fact, HSE encourages everyone who wants to throw a party to go right ahead.

If someone tells you that you can't have a get together to mark the nuptials of Prince William and Kate, then challenge them. Health and safety is about looking out for any legitimate things that might spoil people's fun on the day, not to stop people doing anything at all.

If you want to close a road or are running a party on a commercial basis with alcohol on sale, it's probably a good idea to check with your local council. But in most cases, things like street parties run by volunteers don't have any obligations under health and safety law at all.

Here's to William and Kate!"[51]

This may have shattered a few preconceptions, and left a few sacred cows lying belly up, stunned on the floor. The HSE want to be seen as nice people trying to stop other people dying, not as random restrictors of fun. The 'Myths' section on the HSE website ran for three years, separating fact from legend. It decided to take this approach since it is frequently reported to have 'banned' something - from the game of playground conkers to cheese-rolling. In reality, it has banned very few things outright; one such harmless bit of fun the HSE has banned exclusively is the use of asbestos.

So how did these stories perpetuate? Mainly because some comfortable compromiser *used* health and safety as an excuse not to do something. Perhaps there wasn't the money for the village fête this year because the head of the parish had spent all the budget on a private music recital for his opera society friends, and so blamed the cancellation on the risk of children becoming tangled in bunting. It's far better to blame some far off enemy regulator than your own apathy or incompetence. That isn't to say that Health and Safety isn't at Times over-zealous - but by and large it is concerned with genuine risks to public health. They are more than willing to help you fight your case, and provide a lot of resource on their website to help you win the argument. Unfortunately, the health and safety argument is just one of many, but at least you'll be well on the way to getting your street party up and running.

2. Human Rights

I began my undergraduate studies of law in 2000. In my first ever lecture, we were told that we were the first generation of human rights lawyers, since we were now learning a system which incorporated the Human Rights Act 1998, bringing into British law a consistency with the evolving field of human rights law. Not that it made much difference to my studies from that point on, apart from a standard "of course the Human Rights Act may or may not change this in future" sentence in the lecturer's address, and a standard paragraph to the same effect in every essay.

Human rights law is poorly understood. Most people read scare stories and headlines which seem to suggest that human rights is primarily concerned with providing high-security prisoners with jacuzzis and flat screened televisions in jail. The issue reared its head in the first half of October 2011, when Home Secretary Theresa May made the assertion that the Human Rights Act had allowed the fact that an asylum seeker owned a cat to be a deciding factor in granting him a right to remain in the UK. She was rightly criticised by her party colleague Ken Clarke, who, like many, found the use of such an uncorroborated example by the nation's prime authority on internal affairs to be 'laughable'. The judiciary immediately sprang forth in fury, stating that the cat was not in any way relevant to the decision of the case. This example serves to demonstrate the extremely low regard in which human rights is held; it justifies things we don't want, and opposes things we do want.

In the UK, the main objection appears to be a reaction against the imposition of standards and laws from afar - a set of alien concepts and customs which undermine traditional British values. As with many examples in this book, the truth is a lot more complicated and interesting. The UK has been the birth-place of modern Parliamentary democracy. Its citizens were the first to demand concessions from their monarch in Magna Carta. We were among the first to outlaw the slave trade, give votes to women, and pass public health protection laws. Our constitution is not written down in one place, but it is nonetheless real and enshrines various sacred rights for its citizens. Human Rights Law is an extension of this process, in spirit if not always in execution.

Where rights are written down, the debate around them can become polarised. The gun control debate serves to demonstrate the difficulty of doing anything which can be argued to infringe someone's basic rights. The pro-gun lobby rests on its constitu-tional right to bear arms. Rights and liberties have a very special place of honour in the American collective psyche. You try and reduce an American's freedom at your peril[52]. The pro-gun lobby uses the veneration of the constitution to back its case, linking any attack on gun ownership as a more generalised liberal attack on personal freedom.

A general worry for the future of the world is the 'worship' of rights and rejection of responsibilities. A more litigious culture is emerging, reflects in the tone of daytime TV adverts for no-win-no-fee injury lawyers. The general message communicated to the citizenry is that if you were hurt, it must have been someone else's fault, and you have a right to compensation. An unruly pupil taunts his teacher, decreeing his powerlessness to disci-pline him physically with the phrase "I know my rights".

Rights talk tends to polarise the debate, dividing people among political lines. Importantly it makes a debate seem like an 'ultimate struggle' for your future rather than a negotiation; I have a set of rights which you are seeking to remove, making you a winner and me a loser. Compromise is therefore much harder to achieve. The system of Human Rights law at least creates a context in which legal struggles between conflicting rights and responsibilities can be played out in full view.

3. Europe

The European Union has been the source of many memorable April Fools jokes. Once accused of regulating the curvature of bananas, the redness of tomatoes and the essential Melton Mowbrayness of our pork pies (although the last one is actually true), the general public see the EU and european union law as a mischief, a nuisance which stops us doing certain things. It may stop us marketing our products in a certain way, or protecting ancient crafts. It stops us weighing our groceries in pounds and ounces; it won't let us Brits call our beloved call Dairy Milk 'chocolate' because it doesn't have enough cocoa solids.

It is most criticised as a source of extra administrative burden. When new regulations from Europe come in, it usually means filling out more forms, agreeing to more disclaimers and bothering your clients for more paperwork. European bureaucracy is another external system which may be used to sideline your plan for change. Curiously, the presence of heavy European administrative burden can be used in the past and future tenses - either such regulations exists to stop your plan, or it would require such legislation should it be adopted!

The root of the problem with the EU 'system' is misunderstanding. An appeal to the dominance of a sinister European system is an appeal to a subtle prejudice many will have, as many people with a conservative viewpoint take a generally eurosceptic position. The view has taken hold because people do not understand the role of the European Union, and usually do not see the benefits of it to their own lives. They hear the stories of the bailout of Eurozone economies, of the petty regulation, and they want out. So here follows a potted history and guide to the EU, and why it is pretty much a good thing when you think about it on balance, with apologies to those who think differently.

First, what are its origins? The notion of greater interdependence between the central European states was born in the aftermath of not one but two devastating conflicts. Tensions between France, Germany, Austria and Russia were at the heart of both world wars. The disaster of Versaille, and the penury which the German people were subjected to created the economic poisoning of the Weimar Republic, setting the scene for the emergence of National Socialism. To its major protagonists, the end of World War Two had to come about in such a manner as to ensure future cooperation, not guarantee ongoing antagonism. One way to effect this is was build greater trade links between the countries in question. If these countries were better integrated, if their citizens could trade in a free manner across national borders, finding new markets, everyone would benefit. Domestic producers would be exposed to more competition, yes, but they would also have access to more customers. Citizens would benefit from increased numbers and quality of goods, while integrated governments reliant on each other for economic prosperity would think twice before annexing the Sudetenland or invading Poland. So an integrated Europe is a safer one. The holocaust is still within living memory of a small minority; but our memories are short, and do not appreciate this benefit.

That's the general historical background. How does an actual common market emerge, and what are its key features? Answering this question is vital, since the institutions we need to gain the benefits often lead to the misunderstood consequences referred to above. At its most basic, EU trade law seeks to guarantee certain freedoms - the free movement of good, the free movement of persons and the free right of establishment in another country, for example. Not having to show your passport on your holiday in Europe is surely a benefit, as are the removal of restrictions on duty free goods. This is not to mention the benefit to UK industry from the access to the EU, and the increased investment from foreign firms in UK businesses which were struggling.

It is this trade integration which gives rise to a lot of the misunderstandings. Many see European affairs as a black and white issue - why should a foreign set of politicians have a say in the way 'we run our country'? In fact, the EU brings massive investment into the UK and provides a free market for UK goods - although we don't seem to make many actual goods any more. Those opposed often want the integrated trade, but why should 'they' be able to tell us what we can and can't call a pork pie, or whatever it might be.

The problems lie in the harmonisation of rules, so that trade in goods is truly free. If you were running a market where there was no free movement of goods, you would seek to protect your national industries by a system of tariffs and quotas imposed on foreign goods. You would set a maximum number of foreign imported goods allowed into your home market in order to protect the competitiveness of your home firms' products, or imposing extra taxes on duties on those imported products in order to make them more expensive and hence less competitive than the domestic firms' products. This is known as 'protectionism'. Many developing countries have relied on aspects of this policy to ease their transition. The common market outlaws restrictions on trade which are unfair.

The EU would be much better understood if we just stopped there, but human beings are pretty cunning and like finding ways to get round rules, especially where to do so would bring you a bit of extra income. Countries could effect such protectionism by the back door using rules on quality and ingredients, for example. The early cases in European Union law centred around a French liqueur chocolate being sold on the German market. French law stipulated a much lower alcohol content than

German law in order for something to marketed as a liqueur. Applying German rules to the French product, the chocolate could not be marketed as a liqueur in Germany. The German system demanded much higher standards of quality than the French system. The court in question ruled that this was an unfair restriction on trade. From the French producer's point of view, this makes sense. After all, they have done all they needed to do in their home country to produce and make a sound product, so why shouldn't they be allowed to market it on another market just because of a slight difference in rules? The EU seeks to harmonise such laws in order to make sure they aren't being used to protect domestic goods from foreign competition. German beer purity laws were also attacked. The details are slightly dull; the essence of the cases is this; the existence of local laws stating what 'beer' is, or what can be called a 'Cassis de dijon' liqueur shouldn't prejudice a foreign producers' entry into that market.

So if you work in industry or provide a service, you benefit directly from the effect of such harmonisation laws within the EU. The process of globalisation has created a supra-national economy, one linking geographically far removed countries with ties of mutual dependence. To have such a system, and benefit from it, it stands to reason that we must have some public power which has a remit to deal with such supra-national situations. We cannot deal with trade disputes on a case-by-case basis through bilateral agreements between two parties at anything like the rate and efficiency required. There is a trade off, as certain domestic legislation in the UK will sometimes be beneficial to you, and prejudicial to other member states. We haven't yet solved the problems of a growing EU, and the ructions being sent through the global economy by the Eurozone debt crisis teach us that much work remains to be done to make the system workable and beneficially for most participants.

But taken in the bigger picture, you benefit. Massively. The European project may have lost its way, but its main purpose is to promote peace and prosperity. I realise this may ring very hollow in the midst of the Eurozone crisis, but the single currency project is a separate debate from the single market of which the UK is part. Fundamentally, the EU seeks to assist our global economic development, and as such has adopted certain values and practices. If we don't appreciate these values, we will find ourselves feeling as if the EU has been constructed to deny our success. Learning to play the European game will stand you in very good stead, if you learn the 'language', and decided what concepts you should appeal to when dealing with present or future interactions with the European system.

4. Computers & IT

The information technology (IT) that our place of work or government has adopted to help us execute our tasks is a massive source of systemic malaise, the inspiration for the Little Britain character we looked at back at the start of this chapter. At a national level, we repeatedly hear of failed government agency procurement projects where new IT systems have been implemented over-time and over-budget, only to not work all that well and create more problems through their operation than the old system did.

I have countless anecdotes from my personal struggles with companies over-reliant on their systems, bringing about wasteful and poor results for all concerned. I am a pretty clumsy person, and think it's worth paying extra for insurance on my mobile phones. I dropped my phone and broke the screen a month before I was due for a new contract and an upgrade. I rang the company in question and explained the situation to them. It would have been a big waste of time and resources to use my insurance to give me a brand new phone, only to see me get another brand new phone in a month's time.

Except they couldn't do anything about it. The insurance people were separate from the upgrades people, who didn't work with the contracts people, and in any case, I needed to talk to the repairs people first. The 'computer said no'. Now, this might be just a good example of an especially poorly integrated and run system, but I doubt it. Technology is believed to liberate us, but it can in fact creates barriers and walls to creativity and common sense.

Systems analysts know this is true when they talk of the 'tribal knowledge' which workers within a technologically bounded system develop. Glitches and weird loopholes exists, and the workers develop an ad-hoc library of tricks and manual workarounds to bypass the inefficiencies of the system. The very fact that this knowledge exists may be a source of problems for you. You may be experiencing a problem which does not officially exist, since none of the official manuals sanction the behaviour which is causing you trouble.

The reasons why systems are so infuriating and hence used as a reason to oppose change is due to the way they have evolved. Companies adopt new technologies as and when they become available or commercially feasible. As new products or services are offered, new technologies are adopted and new systems implemented. Equally, as a product fails or a market contracts, systems will be left redundant, under resourced, but sometimes still used occasionally. This leads to most big organisations operating a patchwork of different systems with different operating parameters in different areas. Banks in the UK have suffered from this piecemeal evolution of technological capability[53], first adapting emerging technology in the 1960's with more and more systems having been tacked on over the decades following. Multiple databases lead to doubt and confusion over the 'reality' of the numbers you are trying to deal with. With the vogue for outsourcing, the problem became even more difficult. One bank recognised the need for change, and adopted an investment programme in its IT system in 2008. By this time, the company identified some 55 separate systems for core banking needs and 24 for operating credit cards. Its adoption of internet banking services saw it develop 41 discrete systems. Its easy to see how things might get lost in such a forest of databases, or create the opportunity for subtle opposition to change.

New entrants to the market can adopt new, unified, specially designed systems which bypass all of these problems. If the system entrenched in an existing organisation is hindering change and being blamed for lack of progress, the easiest path is to push for a brand new organisation. Experts in the growth of churches would assert that it is much easier to create a new thing to match modern needs than to try and change something which has operated for years. Non-core issues become sacred to the people who have grown up being used to their dominance. Taking the church example, established congregations in the twentieth century relied on organs and choirs. More recent generations prefer a more pop / folk aesthetic of guitars and drums. The two camps can be at war when a congregation used to the old tries to bring in the new. It can cause a lot of pain and anxiety. It is easier - though not necessarily better - to start a brand new thing where modern values are enshrined from the beginning.

This is an approach which recognises the difficulties of integrating new and old systems, and chooses to deal with it by ignoring it, allowing the new to live and the old to die, and kind of church-growth Darwinism, survival of the 'coolest'. If you find yourself repeatedly opposed by inflexible systems, you do have the option of writing them off entirely, and seeking to invest in the creation of a new system or organisation which can deliver your aim without any need to be hamstring by outdated preferences and ways of doing things. When our physical infrastructure no longer meets our needs, we demolish it and re-build something better with the space we now have. We should take a similar attitude toward our cognitive infrastructure.

Institutional Inertia

There are important lessons to learn from this rather detailed description of four dominant 'systems' in modern life. All of the above suffer from institutional inertia and contribute to it at a societal level. This concept refers not to the lack of ability to adapt to change evident in one organisation (through their computer systems for example), but the collective failure of national and international policy makers and institutions to deal with problems when they are identified, bringing potentially helpful solutions. It is the ultimate example of the system not letting you do something - not just the specific organisation and set of rules you are involved in on a daily basis, but the entire coordinated global system of political institutions.

Once these institutions are in place they tend to show an adhesion, refusing to budge and becoming so enshrined in popular political consciousness that they are unchallenged. As our economies globalise and become more interdependent, so the structures of international governance become more complicated and unwieldy. Institutional change and institutional reform pay off in the long run, however difficult they may be in the short term. If 'the computer says no' then the simple answer is this; talk to the programmer, and change the computer.

Dealing with 'the systems'

A little knowledge goes a long way, and our chapter so far will have given you much needed insight into the peculiarities of the main systems. However, a lot of perseverance goes even further. Many concerned individuals fall at the first hurdle, accepting the first claim that what you want to change is impossible because the system won't let you. Apathy is rather pervasive, and people generally feel that engagement with systems or bureaucracies is futile. However, it only takes a very vocal and passionate few to bring about changes. Reflecting on the work of media watchdog the Advertising Standards Authority, it is amazing to see how few people actually complain about a particular advert which actually ends up being banned. When TV audiences of several million watch an advert which is, for example, too raunchy for a pre-watershed audience, it only takes a few hundred to actually bother to complain for the company in question to be censured. The comfortable compromiser wants you to feel like engaging with the right 'system' wont be worth your effort. But you don't need to persuade millions to take to the streets, often only a few hundred to make the same message. It comes down to the fact that all systems are operated by people who just want to go home as close as possible to 5pm as they can manage. Complaints are hassle, and there comes a point where it's better to deal with them than to be continually nagged.

Dealing with bureaucracy in effecting a change (or even discussing its potential) need not be such a drain on confidence behind your suggestion. There are several tips for dealing with bureaucracies.[54] First, all bureaucracies are different, hence finding the right approach to suit it is vital. Have you found the right person to make a deal with in the first place? You may need to scout the land first, identifying all the organisations involved in the field, to make sure you are dealing with the right people before you begin.

Second, you will need some experience of the organisation in question. This is not something you will likely find through an internet search or in a library, but through someone who has dealt with them before. This might be another company, NGO, consultancy or legal firm. You need to know its status within the territory it is operating in (is it under threat, is it well funded etc.) and the process for making decisions that it has adopted. If the other party appears unstable and lacking in organisational prowess, then a rigorous filing of information and documents amounting to a paper trail will be vital. Not forgetting all the while that there is little substitute for perseverance and patience, as we have seen above.

Finally, we would do well to remember our core assertion, that systems are manifestations of human desires to make work more efficient. If a system is producing an unjust or damaging result, it can be changed, tweaked or re-designed. If a compromiser is using the system surrounding them as an excuse, call them to reassess the suitability of those systems. Stress the injustice and put the pressure on the to justify their continued faith in the systems behind which they are hiding.

If the computer says no, get a different computer - or fire the programmer.

Chapter 7

But Our Statistics Said . . .

When presented with a difficult debate, a common tactic of the comfortable compromiser is to appeal to facts over opinions, usually in the form of the results of statistics or a survey. Numbers, diagrams and percentages are dressed up to make your cause look silly and the status quo look fantastic. Finding out the facts is one of the hardest jobs of the change-agent. However, a scientific approach is now a pre-requisite for any campaign. Using rhetoric and emotionalism can get you so far, and the scientific arena is itself an ideological battleground, but history teaches us that to gain the wider understanding and support of a diverse majority of ordinary people, an appeal to facts is paramount. Social policy academics talk of the need to create a 'policy image' which is a mixture of empirical evidence and emotional appeals.[55] Often the empirical evidence presented can be manipulated to be an emotive appeal in and of itself. Equally, nothing destroys confidence in your cause than sloppy use of evidence, exaggeration and bluster, once discovered. When you are opposing something well established, extra care must be taken to ensure accuracy in your claims, since you will be under greater scrutiny.

Information and the way it is presented is vital because the process of deciding on a course of action is rarely clear cut and simple. We simply cannot know all that we need to about our available time and resources and the realistic effects of our choices on our future. Most of the time, we make do with a rational decision within the boundaries we set for ourselves (the bounded rationality we discussed in chapter three). Making decisions and relating to abstract ideas is a very 'fuzzy' business.

When we introduce numbers, we introduce a clarity into the discussion which is comforting. Or at least, that's what the compromiser wants you to think.

Getting information is vital because of the operation of another of our old friends, the cognitive bias. In this case, we are dealing with the availability bias in dealing with the facts presented to us. We generally believe something to be true when it is presented to us in an easily digestible yet striking and memorable form. When something holds the imagination in this manner, it becomes the central point around which the debate centres, often unfairly or in the face of contrary evidence which was poorly presented. Many of the tactics we are about to delve into in more detail exploit precisely this bias, robing unreliable or incomplete data in a clothing of clarity and ease which leads us to attribute more worth to it than we should.[56]

This chapter seeks to explore how numbers can be manipulated and moulded to create a sense of security which isn't actually there, creating a wide-open space for those with an agenda to run amok with distortions and manipulated data. The dawning of the information age, and the development of mass media and the internet in particular, mean that dealing with numbers is fraught with difficulties. The authority of certain publications is undermined by the blogging and re-tweeting culture which has only very recently developed. Numbers and their interpretation have therefore become an important battleground in public discourse, worthy of the longest chapter of this book.

My parents would daily recommend to me the merits of delayed gratification as I worked my way through formal education. I would encourage a similar view of this chapter. There's a lot to deal with since the excuse is so popular, and we need all the weapons in our armoury we can muster to counter the use and mis-use of 'facts' in public discourse.

"Lies, Damned Lies and Statistics"

Benjamin Disraeli's famous and possibly mythical outburst summarising the three categories of falsehoods echoes with our modern frustration over the use of statistics to mould our views on certain issues. In this section we will explore the basic tool-kit available to someone skilled in the use of statistics to frustrate and obfuscate, but we must first understand the context. Just why are such statistical appeals so powerful, even if the data which undergirds them is dodgy?

Stats played an important role in the American experiment with the prohibition of alcohol. By any stretch of the imagination, the first few years of Prohibition were an unmitigated disaster, as regards any actual prohibition of drinking alcohol. Far from towing the line and being good citizens, people rejoiced in flaunting the laws as a means of demonstrating their liberty. Drinking became the number one social activity, gaining that element of danger which gave it a certain rebellious cache. To take one example,, in New York it was estimated that there were over 30,000 illegal drinking establishments by 1927 - more than twice as many as there were legal premises before prohibition. In 1920, the Internal Revenue Bureau estimated that bootlegging was a business worth over $1bn. Americans consumed an estimated 25m gallons of bootlegged liquor in 1920, combined with the 30m gallons dispenses for 'medicinal' purposes[57].

Yet the Prohibitionists were delighted with the start they made! Wether it be from wilful self delusion or just plain short-sightedness, statistics could be found to show the effectiveness of the policy despite the booming black market. Supporters of Prohibition argued that deaths related to alcoholism had declined in 1920, and other diseases linked to excessive alcohol consumption showed falls in state statistics.

The falls were impressive - but just because they came after the event of prohibition does not mean they were the result of it, the first general lesson for our purposes. The belief of the prohibitionists that their legislation was the cause of the decline in ill-health is a classic example of a logical fallacy best described in Latin:[58]

"Post hoc ergo procter hoc"

This is (very) roughly translated as 'after the thing, therefore because of the thing', describing our difficult relationship with causality. Causality and chronology are two of the most commonly misunderstood concepts in our culture (concepts we will explore more fully in a few pages' time). Not only that, but people do not realise that they are misunderstanding them. We all know that just because things flowed in a particular order doesn't mean that the events preceding the ending caused it, but that doesn't stop us implicitly assuming so for the sake of simplicity. The circumstances often lead us to delude ourselves into believing our own hype. The Prohibitionist in 1922 would have argued against repeal of the legislation - based on interpretation of these 'facts'. Such appeals were continued into the late 1920's, arguing that the 'facts' showed great social benefit, undermined by weak enforcement.

Probability, Causation and Correlation

Why do we care so much about probability and causation in the first place, enough to create confusion over the causes of different events through the creative use and reporting of facts? It is clearly important to establish not just what events came in what order, but whether one event is likely to lead to another. We spend most of time alive deciding which actions to take, and trying to predict or adjust to the actions of others. One of the elements of human consciousness which marks us out from other species is our ability to imagine the impact of our present choices on our individual and collective futures. We can imagine what life would be like if we took a particular action- and we can adjust our present behaviour accordingly. Most marketing people and politicians play on this capacity - inviting us to imagine how positive a future with this party or that product will be, and choosing to take the steps to make it a reality.

If we are reasonably convinced that a specific course of action will have certain results, we will choose to take it, based on past experience - either that which we have enjoyed ourselves, or that which is communicated to us by trusted figures. Every event is caused by multiple factors - so in fact what we are saying is that we believe that one of many partial causes was the most significant in bringing about a particular consequence. If I took a course of medication and got better, I may well try that medication again the next time I have the same symptoms because I attribute an event - my recovery - to one of the many causes of my return to health.

I know this sounds fairly obvious, but this reasoning is often implicit in our day to day lives, and when it comes to making big decisions affecting the welfare of many others, it is important to spell it all out. In making policy decisions, we are deciding to do or not to do something because on the balance of probabilities we think it will cause a desired outcome. Any causation is in fact an observation of a chain of events. It is always an inferred conclusion. Even the most 'obvious' things - touching fire makes me scream with pain - is in fact an observation of a chain of events; we did not specifically see the workings of the central nervous system which detected the extreme heat, sent a message to the brain, which reacted with movements and noise; we observed the reaction, and made the connection.

Sadly, we are not as rational as we like to think we are. All kinds of relevant factors may seem unimportant to us, or irrelevant ones may cloud our judgement. Most people gather their information about the world around them from the mainstream media, who are on the whole notoriously poor at reporting scientific issues. Several other authors do a fantastic job of explaining this is great detail, but the important point for us is to learn how opposition to your plan will be formulated. We have explained how correlations and causality are tricky concepts with much room for ambiguity and assumption which will be played upon by those opposing your intentions. Whether they intend to or not, the media can undermine your case by its reporting on causality.

The word "link" is often used when reporting the results of scientific studies. Readers of a certain daily newspaper in the UK will probably think most foods have some "link" to cancer. The word masks the reality. Imagine the paper reports that there is a link between bowel cancer and eating pre-washed salad. It has not stated that the study proved that eating pre-washed salad causes an increased rate of cancer, only that there is a link. But many will assume than a link is a cause; and the sales of pre-washed salad go down. Of course, the newspaper's motivation is to sell more copies, and so they have a motivation to sensationalise the story.

A statistic demonstrating a correlation does not indicate a causal relationship between two factors. To take some rather silly examples, imagine Jim wishes to join a football club, having moved to a new town. His boots are white, and the majority of the other members' boots are green. He buys green boots, thinking this is a condition of membership, and is confused when his application is refused. He assumed that there was a causal relationship between membership and boot colour; in fact, the football club just got a job lot of green boots from a company that was closing down last year, meaning a lot of people just happen to have green boots.

This is a roundabout way of saying something fairly simple - that even when things seem to be correlated, they may not have any causal relationship, hence the most obvious and 'common sense' intervention may not be the most sensible or effective. Often people will use statistics showing pure correlations and leave the reasoning implicit. It is your job to ask the questions making this reasoning explicit, or conduct a trial which tests the implicit hypothesis.

Let's pretend that you are concerned about a company's management of employment issues. Having communicated this displeasure to the company, they reply stating that all indicators of personal safety performance show a reduction in the number of accidents. The reasoning is implicit - the number of incidents is going down, which must be because of our wonderful management systems. However, there may be all kinds of reasons why the statistics have gone down; the culture may be such that minor incidents are not reported; the kind of work being done may have changed, reducing risk of injury; the number of people employed may have fallen. Or just maybe, the policies are effective. The statistic relied on as a 'key performance indicator' may be inappropriate for the behaviour we are concerned with. If we dig a little deeper, asking questions of implicit and explicit causality we can get past this first hurdle and into a real debate on the company's performance.

Campaigners can be just as guilty of making assumptions of causality from correlations. To take a more controversial example, imagine an area is opened up to mining for the first time. Within a few years, the local community begins to experience a noticeable increase in a particular form of cancer. They suspect that their water supply has been contaminated by the workings of the miners, causing their cancers. They see an 'obvious' chain of causation - more cancers after the mine, therefore the mine caused the cancers. An NGO picks up on the case and begins accusing the company of endangering the health of local people. The company says it has conducted a scientific investigation, and sees no link between its activities and the increase in cancers.

How do we deal with such a situation in an even handed way? What are the possibilities?

1. There is no real increase in cancer rates; prior to the mine, there are inadequate health records.
2. The cancer rate increase is real, but attributed to some other factor.
3. The cancer rate increase is real, but is purely coincidental that it happened after the mine appeared.
4. The cancer rate increase is real, and is caused by the activity of the mining company.

First, we must establish that the events are indeed connected. This is not always easy, as there is the potential for the harm to be new, and not known about previously. Of course, a correlation may have no causal relationship at all. Coincidences do exist, but the context is all important in deciding whether this is the case. An amateur cricket team I have occasionally taken the field for (UBSCC) once fielded an eleven containing no fewer than ten doctors of various academic backgrounds. Among your average village teams, and to the casual inspector of the scorebook it may look like a freak coincidence that ten of the batting line up carried the honorific 'Dr', until you are informed that the acronym stands for 'University of Bristol Staff Cricket Club'. However, we generally want the world to make sense, as it gives life more meaning, hence we tend to read much more into circumstances and chains of events than we ought. This is how conspiracy theories develop, and how scientific research is so poorly reported in the mass media.[59]

The basic statistical tool-kit

Having now understood the relative ease with which beliefs can masquerade as facts, and how trends can be understood as causes, we can now get into the meat and drink of dealing with statistical arguments, and expose the various tactics for manipulating data to make your point. This is a non-exhaustive taster of the kind of techniques which can be used to introduce an air of certainty into an unclear debate. We will now see exactly how our predispositions toward the presentation of data create the opportunity for contrived manipulation.

The baseline year

A very basic question for any data on historical trends is where to start your assessment - what year will you use as the baseline, year 'zero' with which you will compare the next year's performance? Kyoto targets on carbon emissions set the baseline year as 1990, just after the collapse of Communism in eastern Europe and Russia. The timing was important, since the collapse of mass industry produced a massive fall in carbon emissions. Taken from this baseline, Russia has been one of the cleaner countries. If you were to take an oil company's environmental record and base it on a data set from just after a major disaster it would look much better than if the year before it was also included.

This is a very basic level of data manipulation, and if done crudely is all to easily detected. But that doesn't stop people doing it. The classic trick is to zoom in or zoom out. If you progress has been incremental, a 10 year graph will show your performance as weak. A three year graph will show good progress. If there has been a massive increase year on year in an indicator, zoom out over 20 years and it will look like an anomaly. Crude, but effective.

Normalising

Normalising is the process of relating data to another subset of data in order to make its assessment more meaningful. Classically, this involves not looking at 'raw' consumption data, say for example, the amount metal used by a factory in a year, which may go up and down according to demand, production and the size of the organisation, but normalising this data against some other factor, perhaps throughput, turnover or number of employees.

Companies like to use this approach when assessing their performance on air emissions. Carbon emissions generally rise as a company grows, since they use more energy. A booming industry may well wish to report on its carbon emissions, but would not want to report that its emissions have gone up by 10% each year for the last 5 years. Instead, you wish to communicate that you emissions relative to the cost of production have in fact gone down incrementally. If you divide the raw figures by the total operating costs, you come up with a figure of carbon emissions per tonne of finished product. This may show that you have in fact become more efficient producer of your product, since you emit a percentage smaller amount of carbon per unit produced.

This is fairly sensible on an individual basis. Clearly some issues lend themselves towards normalising more than others. Health and safety statistics need to be normalised to be of any use as an indicator. If you operate in a relatively dangerous industry where there is a daily risk of minor injury, such as waste handling, you may see around 500 accidents a year out of 1,000 staff. If you see major redundancies, and the headcount falls to 500, then your umber of accidents would fall by perhaps 50%. If you don't normalise this data, it is easy to present it as a vastly effective safety campaign which has cut the incidents of workplace injury in half, while all that has really happened is that half the number of people were at risk of getting injured, and the process itself is no safer than it ever was. In this case, you would be sensible to normalise it against the headcount, and come up with an indicator that reflects the overall level of risk to your staff, such as the number of accidents per hours worked.

In these cases, normalising is reasonable. However, the nature of the problem and the necessary solutions are the key deciding factors in assessing the suitability of normalising in presenting data. The carbon emissions problem is absolute. There is a finite amount of carbon which the whole ecosystem can tolerate in the atmosphere and regulate within its capacity. If is not a relative problem. It really wont matter if every human activity improves its carbon efficiency by 10%, but the whole of industry grows by 15%, in which case we've still emitted more carbon overall. Normalising our emissions can create the illusion of progress, making us feel OK about our approaches to the issues while the underlying problem is getting worse not better. When working with normalised data in your discourse, the nature of the problem is your starting point.

Comparisons

In his recent stand-up material, the Welsh comedian Rhod Gilbert makes an emotional plea for equal treatment of the Welsh people by the newscasting community. Why, he asks, whenever there is a disaster anywhere in the world do research teams compare the area affected to the size of Wales?

There are enough things and phenomena in the world to provide a limitless source of comparisons for numbers. Since we struggle to cope with complexity and abstract concepts, especially when the material is unfamiliar, it is often helpful to make a comparison to something more common place, so people can get a handle on an unfamiliar issue. But this can often be a source of intentional obfuscation, since our automatic thought processes help us understand issues based on our prior experience - our framing (See chapter three). Since we typically struggle to make sense of information quickly without reference to its context, which context we are guided to is critical.

A very basic manipulation involves comparing big numbers and small numbers. If I'm trying to get you worried about something, I will use a bigger number than if I'm trying to get you to feel good about it. Which units I use will be very helpful in setting the context for my argument.

Let's pretend someone is trying to open a whiskey distillery and intends to use a local spring as a source of water. Someone concerned about the project may make the following kinds of statements. For the sake of the example, let's assume that all parties are telling the truth:

"The distillery will use several million litres of water a year"
"The distillery will use the equivalent of 1,000 households' daily water use each year"

Taken by themselves those statistics seem worrying. I may not know much about water supplies and what is or isn't a significant amount of water to take from a stream, but I know that a million is a big number, and therefore I might be worried. That's a reason why the second statement works - I can make the link between the water used by the distillery and the equivalent 'lost' to household consumption. The context has made me worried about two things - the size of the project, and the risk to my own water supply.

How would comparisons be used by someone who wants to reassure you? Our fictional distillery owner will make the following kinds of statements, which will frame your view very differently:

"The distillery will use only 0.5% of the spring's total daily flow volume"
"The distillery will use 50% less water per bottle of whisky produced than other distilleries in the area"

If I encounter these statistics first, I see the distillery as a small business with a tiny impact on the community, and one which is much better than others which might be operating in the area. There are several issues here. Firstly, you may be an expert on aquatic ecosystems, but let's assume you aren't, like the majority of people. You don't have the expertise to know what abstracting 0.5% of a river's flow will do the life which it supports - human, plant and animal. But crucially, you do know that 0.5% is a very small proportion. If my food was only 0.5% fat, I would eat it on my diet. If the price of milk went up 0.5% I would probably not notice. Importantly, I use my understanding of other issues and contexts in which a small percentage makes no difference, and I automatically assume that this is true in the current context (ring any bells?). This is why comparisons are helpful and dangerous in the same breath.

The second issue comes with the comparison to the other producers. This is also playing with the context, but in a subtly different way. Instead of making us draw on experiences from potentially irrelevant areas of our past experience, this statistical comparison draws us into the specific context on distilleries. It makes me feel confident that things are worse in other companies, and at least this one will be having a proportionally smaller than some other unlucky souls are undergoing. It subliminally limits the discussion to the narrow topic of distillery efficiency; wider discussion of the impact is therefore precluded, since we are talking about distilleries.

Thee tactics are fairly commonplace, and both sides of a debate pick and choose the statistical comparisons which suit them best. The first step is to analyse the argument, and discover the premise on which the statistical point is resting. So in the example above "The distillery will use only 0.5% of the spring's total daily flow volume", we can break it down as follows:

1. The distillery will use 0.5% of the spring's flow in a day
2. This is so small a number that the spring will be unaffected.
3. Therefore the distillery will not affect the spring in any meaningful way.

The use of the statistic rests on point 2; this is the assumption that is intended to go unnoticed. Assuming the statistic is factually accurate, and you have no reason to doubt that the impact will be less or more than 0.5% day, your questions should focus on 2. What evidence do they have to support their (implicit) contention that relatively small abstractions do not affect springs? It may be worth consulting your own experts on this point, to give you the ammunition to start the questioning.

Whole number bias

In our cognitive tool set which we use to make decisions, we have an odd subliminal preference for whole numbers. If asked to guess a number, our first estimates will be round numbers, since we are immersed in the decimal system. It's not just that we prefer to guess whole numbers (the actual process of guessing a number relies on using whole numbers- our initial ball park figure is round, then we decide if it's higher or lower, we use whole numbers as the mid point). A good rule of thumb when considering estimates given to you in numerical form is that 'the rounder the number the less is known about the subject matter'.[60] Of course, knowing this, you now have the opportunity to massage your round number into a more specific one, purely to give the impression that you know much more about a subject that you do. If you suspect someone of using this tactic, ask for the detailed figures, so that you can work them out for yourself.

Dodgy data

Of course, the data may not be manipulated in any statistical sense; it may just be plain wrong. A system of data collection may be weak, resulting in accurate data being collected and attested as true. Usually such issues only present themselves when the collection process is flawed to begin with. For example, a water treatment works may need to report on the emission of a certain chemical into a local river. If it has set up a flowstation with a monitoring box to check for a chemical in the water, and the threshold is zero, a perfectly function monitoring box and a broken one will return the same result, even if the reality is different. What is needed is a failsafe device, one which will assess the problem from another angle, one which will capture the data in a way to tell you when the monitoring device or system is flawed.

There is always the risk of active tampering, of course. The monitoring may well be working fine, but the results are transcribed by human agents who are under pressure from different sources to manipulate the results to fit their needs. These are small examples, but the criticisms ring true for larger issues. If the data seems to be against you, challenge its collection method and look for the existence of checks and balances to correct any mistakes

Diagrams

Once we've played around with choosing our statistic, set our units and decided on the most appropriate time frame, we move into the next stage, that of how to represent this 'fact' to the world. This is equally important as any previous step in the process, and the right diagram or graphical representation can often be the difference in gaining widespread awareness of your case or campaign.

Diagrams have immense power that words do not possess on their own, especially when it comes to reducing complex ideas into easy-to-understand concepts. There has been a burgeoning interest in the graphical representation of data in recent years, as many champion the functional use of graphics to make statistical points. The power of a good diagram has been well understood for a much longer time than that. By no means the earliest example of a diagram causing ripples in civilisation, but certainly one of the most controversial came with the publication of "The revolutions of the heavenly spheres" by Copernicus in 1543. In amongst pages of text and calculations outlining the basis for his theory was a simple drawing, with the planets orbiting round the sun in circular 'orbits'[61]. Copernicus knew that the orbits of the planets weren't so perfect, but since he was more interested in establishing proof for the classical notion of 'uniform circular motion' of the planets, this is how he chose to show his findings. But the power of the diagram is in its simplicity. The Earth, and the creatures living on it, are not the centre of the universe.

Diagrams combine our sense of sight with our rational under-standing, but we do not view such images in neutral terms. Instead, we bring to them all of our past understanding and prejudice. Investment professionals such as myself generally like things going up - profits, dividends, earnings. We really don't like it when things go down. It was once suggested to me that this was a psychological reason why many in the profession struggled to come up with the energy to develop a strategy for achieving cuts in carbon emissions. All the graphs show a problem increasing which we need to decrease, shown in terms of graphs and their lines projecting a necessary downward trend. Maybe if we flipped the graphs over we would get more buy in, by showing the problem in terms of the size of the cuts needed rather than the overall emissions which needed to be reduced. The graph goes up as we track the size of the cuts made, and we feel happier.

Equally, a diagram can be profoundly effective when used against you, undermining your case, helping your opponent to gloss over the issues and present itself in the most favourable light. An energy company once ran a series of adverts telling the world about their approach to cleaner energy. They adopted a small logo for each of the energy sources they were involved in - oil, gas, solar, wind and biofuels. The message of the adverts was that the company was making significant investments in alter-native energy. The logos were shown in order, as a sum, adding up to a clean energy future. As a diagram it seems reasonable, but the implication was that the company was equally involved in all areas. In reality, the solar and wind businesses were tiny compared to the gas business, which in itself was pretty small compared to the oil exploration and production business. An effective strategy to counter such use of material where you think the underlying facts have been mis-represented is to use the image for your own purposes, and re-size it. So in this case, an NGO may have taken the graphics and reproduced the adverts showing the relative sizes of the business units in real terms.

Capturing opinions

Having spent some time looking at the general nature of stats, facts and beliefs, we are more aware of the need for good information in making decisions between different alternative actions. An extra element to consider when making such decisions is the preference of society. These attitudes or opinions are also reported in a factual, numerical manner which is open to manipulation.

Opinion polls hold a rarefied position in modern policy and political discussion. The majority of people assume that polls are the best way of finding out what people really care about, and believe them to be a crucial part of the democratic machine, since they are inclusive of all views. There certainly are rigorous, detailed, balanced public opinion polls which we rightly rely upon to help inform our decisions, but there are also a growing number of 'nonscientific and often biased polls conducted by private and public groups through a variety of mechanisms . . .often confused with legitimate public opinion polling' (Asher). The power of good polling is exactly what the pseudo-polls try to exploit, and serve to justify a little more reflection.

We perceive polls to be scientific and objective, and the commissioners of the polls to be neutral, disinterested observers of the results. We assume that the poll is value neutral, and seeks to merely reveal the preferences and values which people already hold. However, many thinkers on the issue of policy formation consider the truth to be that 'values do not exists in a decision maker's mind; rather they may be moulded or formed during an assessment procedure that seeks to elicit them'[62]. Our values may be vague and general. None of us really have time to think in depth about every issue which affects our lives, whether it be questions about taxes, the welfare state or the existence of a divine being. Our experiences and upbringing will have lead us down very different paths. Our understanding and values in some areas will be much more developed than in others, purely by virtue of the fact that the issues have been thrust upon us to think about. If not, our values are ripe to be moulded and manipulated, artificially and prematurely condensed into actual choices by the survey or poll procedure.

The value of a poll in drawing conclusions about people's beliefs rest on three very important elements - the questions, the sample size and techniques and the interview method. Failure to be objective in any of these steps can skew a result, while people will assume the poll to be accurate and balanced. But before this, the commissioning of the survey will decide its character. If we are in business and about to launch a new product, we may wish to do some sampling of the population to find out what our potential market may be. Here we have an incentive to be balanced and fair, as we do not wish to risk our financial ruin on rose-tinted visions of our customer base. The problem comes when other groups commission surveys 'not to address a public concern scientifically and objectively but to promote a certain position and to convince the public of the rightness of that stand', to quote the guru on the issues of good polling, Asher. The core elements of survey - the questions, the sample and the interview technique - can all be constructed in such a way as to mould people's views in particular directions, and harness their preconceptions and background.

Questions

All surveys are not created equal. They can be rigorous or sloppy, reliable and unreliable. What makes a good survey, and how can you know when the results of a survey are being manipulated in a manner prejudicial to your cause? Then, is the core assertion of the result of the survey accurate? Did it really measure what it set out to measure - essentially, did the survey being quoted ask the right question? In helping us decide whether this is the case, we need to distinguish between the measured property and the target property; usually they are different things, especially when one is conducting surveys into intangibles (which they will be by definition if you are looking for proxy indicators of behaviours, trends or attitudes).

There are several features of a survey which may make its results untrustworthy, and hence should be avoided by you if you choose to use surveys, and pointed out by you if a survey's results appear to argue against you. Firstly, what people say to a surveyor and what people think can be different. People can be intentionally dishonest, or just inconsistent through human frailty. For example, if the questions are trying to find out your attitude on very controversial issues, one where you may not be prepared publicly what you believe in private, you may choose to lie, especially if the survey is conducted in public. In this case, you must ask how the survey has been designed to remove the risk of this error.

Second, the questions themselves can lead people to give answers which do not reflect the true situation. Generally, we do not wish to look foolish and inconsistent in our answers, and this leaves an opportunity for exploitation. Firstly, an individual question may be loaded; then the entire flow of questioning may lead you towards a particular answer. This works because our values and views in many areas are general and not specific. The questions can lead us into concrete views which we may not really hold.

Surveys are often used by companies to justify support for controversial projects, usually those which have national benefits but significant local impacts. While wider stakeholder groups may be concerned, surveys will show that a certain percentage, usually a majority, of local people are in favour. The headline figure deserves scrutiny. In my own experience, a company relied on a survey to state that a public transport project in a disputed territory enjoyed support across a divided community. We asked to see the survey, and asked who it had been conducted by. Since neither details were forthcoming, we could not rely on the findings. It's easy to imagine a crude character of such a survey; pick lots of things most people are in favour of, and lots of things people don't like. You can make it hard for people to disagree with you:

"Do you think your community would benefit from significant financial investment?"

"Do you think your community would benefit from being better connected to the wider city?"

"Do you think local issues should be decided by local people?"

"Are you in favour of the proposed project?"

Now, opposing it would need a person to say that they don't want investment, they want to be isolated, and they want to be dictated to from above. So they will naturally support these statements, leading them to more naturally support the project. This is known as the 'question effect'. The questions 'force the respondents into a world which has little real meaning for them' (Asher). These questions and examples are a little fatuous and assume that the constructer has a particular axe to grind. Such obvious examples would probably be detected by the reasonable man responding to them. But even if this is not the case and the surveyor wants to be balanced and fair, the wording and order of the questions is still hugely important.

So far we've dealt with simple 'yes / no' questions and seen how they can be manipulative. But we're only just getting started on how questions in surveys can be constructed to give a higher probability of a desired result. Multiple choice questions are also very useful to the unscrupulous pollster, since they can provide false choices. If you want someone to endorse your issue as the most important - say, climate change - you will include it in a list of relatively unimportant factors. Most people would pick climate change against a list of more trivial environmental factors. If the survey comes out and says "80% of people consider climate change to be the most important issue facing the world", we must ask what options they were given in the first place. If the list included defence, immigration and economic security, then we would listen. If it included free school milk, advertising standards and alcohol licensing we may not be as ready to shout the results from the rooftops.

A question can be constructed to look on the surface as if it is asking one question, when in fact it is asking two. The classic mentioned by Asher is this - "Do you still beat your spouse?" Or "have you stopped using illegal drugs?" The question is actually asking for two pieces of information, regarding your past conduct and current behaviour. It may force an unwitting responder who only skim reads the questions into admitting, possible falsely that he beat his wife of took drugs. The solution is simple; ask two separate questions, and discount the results of surveys which are not specific in their focus.

Generally, the more specific a question, the more reliable to result. If a question is ambiguous, it is less helpful. Double negatives again provide the possibility for opinions to be misrep-resented, using wording to create doubt about what target property the questions is in fact trying to get at. So we might ask "Do you agree or disagree that the holocaust never happened?" and get a very different set of results than if we asked people straight out. Therefore, questions must be pretested to ensure their effectiveness. So, use of the terms 'recently' or 'in the last few years' will be interpreted differently by different people. Again, this is clearly an opportunity for your opponent to exploit if his intentions are sinister, but even if they are not the use of ambiguous terms can affect the survey.

Another useful trick to marginalise an issue is to use open ended questions in a survey. These do not use the emotional cues to load the question as we have discussed above, giving people a yes or no option. Rather they ask people to name what they think is the most important factor. Using the issue of gun control in the United States as a testing ground, we might ask people what they think the most pressing problem facing the country is, or for their suggestions in how best to deal with crime. Some studies show that in such situations where the subject has to sum up their entire philosophy on what is 'wrong' with society and how best to fix it, gun control is only mentioned by around 11% of respondents as an important issue, and less than 1% think dealing with it would reduce crime. The anti-gun control lobby loves these surveys. You can trot them out on talk radio and breakfast news, claiming easily that there are far more important things to be getting on with, since 89% of people are more worried about other things.

The result of the survey is not the problem here, but the interpretation. In asserting the result, we make the assumption that the evidence of this survey is conclusive, but that might not be the case. I may have conducted in depth research into gun control, considered all the options and come out strongly and consistently in favour of it, and yet still not consider it the 'most important' issue in dealing with crime rates. Knowing this, you must swiftly attack the premise of the argument being backed up by the survey. The user of the stat is hoping that people will automatically assume the survey is fair and balanced, and interpret the percentage in favour result in the usual way; large good, small bad. Even better, they will use the stat in their conversations with others, and these other parties will hear the stat and accept it as gospel, not knowing anything about its basis construction or bias. Open ended questions do not provide enough insight into how strongly people feel about the issue concerned. They ask people to generalise about what they think the priorities should be, with all the same problems of ignorance and cost of expressing our opinion that we've already covered.

Finally, the questions should be constructed to take account of 'response instability'. We have seen that opinions are easily manipulated by the wording of questions and the order in which they come, but out attitudes to different issues can also be variable over a short time scale, which is probably not representative of how most people's attitudes shift and evolve. In short, my responses may not be consistent and may be unstable. I may give contradicting responses in different parts of the survey, and the unscrupulous pollster can pick the result which most suits his purposes. A key requirement of a balanced survey is that answers to complicated issues should be assessed from multiple angles using a number of survey questions, not just one or two false choices between the issues.

The Sample and Technique

How can a sample size of a few thousand accurately represent the entire population of tens of millions? People often distrust this stage of a poll outright, since they cannot conceive of how this extrapolation can ever be valid. Many people will have never been contacted by a pollster, and so will doubt whether anyone they know has either. Asher gives us two good analogies - my doctor needs only a fraction of my blood to see how healthy I am, and a chef needs only to taste a spoonful of the soup to see how well the whole thing is progressing. So a sample of a population can be representative - if done properly.

There is a real issue of perception which will be of interest if you use surveys to back up your points, as opposed to being attacked with them. The problem is that while many put too much faith in surveys, a similar number place no faith in them whatsoever. A sample of about 1,500 Americans can speak pretty well for a population of 200 million. Bizarrely, at least on the face of it, the same size sample is adequate for a much smaller regional state population. These facts seem to many to be anomalies, and undermine many people's faith in the entire exercise.

Understanding stats to a degree level would help, but I don't have that level of education; so I summarise Asher's very helpful analogies of the blood test and the soup tasting once again. Why is this? Mainly because one small drop of my blood has properties identical to the rest of the blood in my body. My company doctor has identified over several years that I have naturally high levels of a hormone related to digestion. He is right to surmise that the few drops of blood he took last year were not taken from a randomly 'patchy' concentration of this hormone, but accurately represent the composition of my blood. The properties of the soup and whether it needs more salt are reliable for the whole pot, provided it has been stirred enough. Similarly, a sample of a few drops of water will tell us whether pollutants are present in a river or stream, provided they do not take the drops from directly underneath an effluent drainage pipe. So it is with sampling of opinions.

Firstly, how will you select people to become part of your sample? The gold standard for drawing a sample from a population is 'probability sampling', as opposed to non-proba-bility samples, where people are included in the survey on the say-so of the sampler. When probability sampling has been used, we can assess the probability of any one person being selected for the survey. Straw polls on street corners beloved of consumer news programmes are non-probability surveys, as are radio text-ins. The alternative is random sampling - where every member of a given population was just as likely to be called upon to respond to the survey as any other. Simple sampling is easy. You have a list of the population, given them a number and randomly select participants.

However, this isn't useful when sampling something large like the population of the UK. How can you be sure your list is correct and up-to-date? So samplers use a variant - systemic sampling; you pick the first name at random, and then every 'nth' name from the list. You could use characteristics to 'stratify' the potential participants - say, by political allegiance or race. You could perform 'cluster' sampling, conducting multiple interviews in an area. The variants are practically endless. But the method most often used in national polls is telephone sampling. They are fast and reactive, and cheap to conduct, hence they are much beloved of politicians. There are issues with phone sampling such as fatigue, but generally people who do respond are less hostile since their personal physical space has not been invaded. Generally, penetration of telephone lines has increased, meaning that there is less of an effective of selection bias towards people rich enough to have a phone.[63] However, you can see how the method of interview may affect your responses. If someone physically comes to your door and disturbs your progress through the latest box-set, you may be angry and desire to get things done with quickly, in which case you just answer without really thinking, if you answer at all. Where and how an interview is conducted is crucially important in assessing the validity of a survey.

What size sample do you need? The size of sample will likely be determined by how much sampling error you are prepared to live with. By sampling error we mean the difference between the results gained from the sample, and that of the general population. Consider a national poll of the leaders of a party which claims that 55% of people support the current Prime Minister or president the sampling error may be 4%, based on the confidence we have in the data from the size of the sample that we could afford to make in a proper fashion. This means that between 51% and 59% of people actually support the leader. If we want to reduce the error, we can spend more money and sample more people. Obviously, the size of the sampling error will be more important when the issue is more finely balanced. If 90% of people think the fresh faced leader of the government is the best thing since sliced bread, the a sampling error of 4% is irrelevant. Finally, the more you break down a result into sub-group, the bigger your error. The margin might be 4% for all UK citizens; but could you say the same when speaking for the opinion of all lesbian, white trades unionists?

Even if we know the sample size - 1,500, in the example above - then we need to be aware that not all of the 1,500 will answer every question. Every percentage in the results does not carry the same weight. So we might be sampling people about the level of road tax, and only 80% of the sample drive a car. The sample has shrunk, and thus the sampling error for this question rises. This again gives rise to the risk of playing fast and loose with the facts. We could construct three questions, the first two of which whittle down the original sample. So we ask if you have a licence, which gives us 80% or 1,200 respondents. We then ask if you have two or more cars in the household, which halves the sample again, to 600 respondents. We then ask this subset of the original 1,500 what their views on raising environmental taxes on vehicle fuels are. Not only is there some selection bias (as two car households will likely be richer), but the sampling error will have increased dramatically. It would be "misleading and unscrupulous to release only the results of the last item without the necessary qualifiers"(Asher). This doesn't stop people doing precisely that in order to give a misleading impression of the level of support for their position.

Pollsters do have some techniques available to them to adjust the sample for the bias they have encountered, and for the scrupulous operators it is actually in their interests to do so.

Biases in the sample are dealt with by weighting. If we feel our randomly selected 1,500 sample has too few ethnic minorities compared to then general population, we may assign a greater value or 'weight' to responses by ethnic minorities in the results, or reduce the effect of the non-ethnic minority respondents. Such efforts can appear to be 'gerrymandering' to the uninitiated, but they are in fact an expression of the desire for the results to be the best and most reliable they can be. On the face of it, people in love with 'one man, one vote' notions of democratic freedom may display knee-jerk responses to weighting, but you are now in a position to help them see that they are legitimate and necessary to get the right result. There are problems, of course, since we assume that the sample of ethnic minorities we are giving extra weight to are in fact representative of the rest of the subgroup, but this is represented in an increased sampling error, so at least- we are aware of it. If you have conducted a survey, be prepared to answer questions about your sampling; if it's being used against you, bring the issue into the open.

Pseudo Polls

Most interviews in polls are a trade off between accuracy and the cost of ensuring that accuracy. The best way of getting useful opinions from people is to pay trained interviewers in one-on-one interviews, but these are expensive. Self-administered surveys such as mail shots have the advantage of hitting lots of people for low costs, but face problems of determining who exactly responded. Internet polls should be able to help some of these shortcomings, since they can reach a large number of people relatively cheaply.

The biggest problem with internet polls is that respondents are not selected through a rigorous scientific procedure aimed at producing a balanced sample. Instead, they are self-selecting to greater or lesser degrees. Only the most interested, most opinionated and in some cases the most bored at work will respond to the survey. Even if a poll is well-constructed and balanced, what website it is hosted on will be a source of selection bias. We would not be shocked that 90% of visitors to 'whitesupremacist.co.uk' thought immigration policies were too weak, nor would we be surprised that readers of 'homeschool-ingmums.org' thought family values would be the most important issue in the next election. Multiple respondents make a mockery of a poll (although steps can be taken to prevent multiple votes), as do mass media campaigns. How else do we explain 80's throwback Rick Astley winning best breakthrough artist at the MTV music awards? An online survey in the wake of the financial crisis and deficit reduction strategy in the UK recently shows this rather wonderfully; when asked "Do you support the elimination of unnecessary non-jobs in the public sector?" an overwhelming 95% were in favour; which raises the terrifying possibility that 5% of people think unnecessary non-jobs are a good thing.

Internet surveys are not hopeless causes. The important thing is to deal with the self-selection issue, so that you get a chance of a sample with which you can estimate the probability that it actually represents a group. The worst polls are pure enter-tainment - do you think the England football manager will be sacked on <u>guardian.co.uk</u>, for example - but there are popula-tions of people where lists exists and you can be sure you've sampled the population. A large employer may have 1,000 email users, in which case they will know with some certainty which people have responded, and what their sampling error is. A university may be similarly appropriate for using email and internet surveys.

Mushy opinions, mushy thinking

There are large tomes written on the subjects of opinion polling which we have done a little to summarise here. I hope you get the picture, and do not feel daunted when the opinion polls seem to be against you. Dig deeper, and ask the questions we've outlined. As a general rule, if you can't see the questions, don't know the sample or can't assess the questioning technique, then you cannot say for sure whether the survey is reliable. In the case of the public transport project, the company would not share the questions, the sample or the techniques. For all we know they could have asked the one member of the population most likely to benefit from the project who had internet access what his opinion was, while offering him a substantial cash reward. They quickly withdrew the survey from their website; I leave you to draw your own conclusions regarding the quality of the survey from this highly anecdotal and circumstantial evidence, from a sample of one. All of this could have been avoided if the company was able to dissociate itself from the survey. We would have been much less concerned about the questions and the sampling if the survey had been commissioned by someone genuinely independent.

However, these issues are well know to those in the field, and attempts have been made to assess the shortcomings of polls and correct for them. This has resulted in the pleasantly entitled "Mushiness index" of Yankelovich, Skelly and White. This assesses the volatility of the public's answers on different issues, especially where people answer even though they may be uninformed. It looks at how much an issue affects them personally, how well informed they feel, how much they discuss the issue with friends and family, and their own assessment on the likelihood of them changing their mind. It categorises their responses on a scale from mushy to firm - general domestic issue attitudes were less mushy.

Taking a somewhat tangential meander into amateur philosophy, the biggest problem caused by over-reliance on polls is that it can *replace genuine thought*. It can lead you into blind alleys, and down roads the pollster wanted you to, certainly, but it also subtly limits your options, weakening your imagination.

Gertrude Stein observed this phenomena - stating that the "funniest" thing ex-pats in Paris 'discovered' about America after WW2 was the Gallup opinion poll.

"When a man can take a poll and tell what everybody is thinking, that means nobody is really thinking anymore".[64]

"Let 'em have it!"

Let's pretend you've been through a protracted battle to get at the real information on an issue. You've challenged the comfortable compromiser's assumptions, samples and surveys with all your energy and passion. When you have been calling for more information and improved disclosure, your target has one more weapon in his arsenal; let you have it. All of it. Every scanned page, every email, every telephone conversation. While you do nothing but deal with this information dump, the debate is suspended as your efforts are sidelined. This seems a positive step, until you realise that the parties often have vastly unequal capacity and resource at their disposal. It also shifts the onus off the compromiser, who can now proudly boast that it has 'achieved full disclosure', and puts the pressure back on those making complaints to change their tactics.

Fortunately, the shifts in global telecommunications technology offer us a counter to this step. Using websites and social media, we can 'crowd-source' the research into the information. In 2011, the 'wikileaks' website made available a vast array of US Embassy communications, far too many for the associated press agencies and journalists to deal with in a short space of time. Most of the more progressive websites and newspapers issued an appeal for help from their readership. Through their websites, newspapers have developed an element of online community which can be used as a resource. Recruiting a few thousand volunteers to help you sift through the information has proved very fruitful. Crowd-sourcing has also been used to great effect in conducting collaborative research, or transcribing ancient documents.

This chapter wouldn't be complete with a final word about the medium where most public debate of statistics and information is conducted - the media. The average journalist lives in a world where deadlines are everything, and any source of easy copy will be lapped up. Reporting on an issue, a journalist is unlikely to have done his own in depth research, but will be repeating back the arguments of the most compelling person he or she talked to that day about the issue. Pressure groups, NGOs, industry bodies and think-tanks will all feed their interpretations of stats to their media contacts.

Mark Damazer (Master of St Peter's College, Oxford, and a former controller of Radio 4) has a long involvement with news reporting, and has highlighted the dangers of journalists relying on information being fed to them to make their stories.[65] Meaningless statements such as 'petrol prices reach record levels' come in for particular criticism. The overall price may be higher than it's ever been - but what of inflation? What matters is whether the price of petrol has gone up or down relative to average incomes or the wider cost of living. Writing in the Guardian he stated:

"Curiosity about data matters. Journalists and their editors should challenge more loudly and more often those who make daft claims based on dodgy statistics. It will take time to get rid of data debris, but we would all benefit."

The media have the capacity to misrepresent the findings of a study or poll, mainly by way of a narrow focus on one element of a study. Polls themselves and their results often form the news, sponsoring polls into issues to create their own headlines. Again this is either something you will choose to exploit or to challenge. Getting your discipline or subject well reported in the press is notoriously difficult. However, most people don't get past the first hurdle; they assume that if they have a strong case and make it with good data, it will be heard. In reality, good information does not 'attract' an audience. It needs to be 'pushed' out, and how you push it out will define how well you are heard.

Factual claims and generalised criticisms

The final stage on our brief tour through the murky world of statistics involves our own use of such data, and the rhetorical devices which can be used in debates on the factual basis of our concerns. A lazy argument against your factual claim is a generalised criticism. If you are making a claim on one hand, for example, a claim that all members of a class of people possess a certain characteristic - blue eyes, say - then a sound argument against the proposition is that Bob has green eyes.[66] However, such criticism often comes in generalised form - a response saying "well, you don't know that; somebody might not have blue eyes". Sometimes this is valid, but often it is a knee-jerk response. Your next step is to ask for specific example, which you can then deal with. The other way to deal with this situation is to avoid it entirely, and not make such a concrete, all encompassing statement in the first place.

It is possible to make a generalised criticism based on the possible existence of evidence to disprove a factual claim in *every* situation. Often in direct debates on television or in the radio, this kind of generalised criticism is made, since it sounds valid to the listener, but in reality it makes no actual point. Merely pointing out the possibility of the existence of doubt should not undermine your argument, but unless you're careful, it will. Go on the attack immediately and ask for specific examples. Human imagination is powerful, and its possible to come up with any number of plausible scenarios which may speak against your factual claim. But would it be sufficient to deny your claim that smoking causes increased incidences of cancer and heart disease by saying that 'some smokers live to 100'? Even if we were to find the name and address, birth and death certificates of the smoker, and proof that he smoked a significant each day, the individual experience does not prove the rule. You need to bring the debate back the specifics.[67] Where is your data showing that smokers have long lives, because the premise of your argument is that because some smokers live linger, smoking doesn't cause harm?

This is the golden rule for dealing with factual debates; uncover and expose the fundamental premise on which the factual claim is made. This the one major reason why we place too much value on factual claims which appear to speak with logic and dispassionate clarity into a difficult debate. Most modern deliberations on policy or choices facing individuals are simply not that simple. Anyone presenting such issues as straightforward is usually masking complexity for the sake of an easy, comfortable life. Become well acquainted with statistics and surveys and you will be much better placed to deal with the compromiser's excuses, getting them out of the way early on, moving the debate into much more productive territory.

Chapter 8

But We're Not The Right People

The final two chapters deal with a very troubling stage of public discourse. Imagine that the debate over the issues is all but over, and the people you need to convince have been persuaded of the merits of a particular change. We now need to move from under-standing the problem to agreeing the implementation of solutions. These two excuses are all about action, and you can be certain that the comfortable compromiser in your midst will make an appeal to either one or both of our final excuses. The first standard excuse in this familiar situation is this; "But we're not the right people".

The response admits that 'situation x' is concerning, and that something should be done about it. However, it's someone else's problem. Or if it really is their problem, they don't have the resources, expertise, authority or time to deal with it. They may suggest that you speak to someone they know who can actually help you. The tactic's negative effects are then compounded when the person you have been recommended to talk to about 'situation x' claims exactly the same thing - yes, it's concerning, but you really need to talk to the people in charge. You end up being pushed round and round in circles, bounced from department to department. Years can pass, and vital energy is wasted as you concentrate all your efforts on keeping up with the buck as it is rapidly passed around.

In general, when you've encountered the body you think should be concerned to deal with your argument, and they have accepted the case but don't want to do anything about it, they have two options. They can go up or down the hierarchy. Here is a rough attempt to sketch out such a hierarchy, which should hopefully be reasonably familiar:

THE TOP
WHO, UN, WTO, UN Organisations, IMF, supranational regulators, International NGOs
Trade and political unions - NAFTA, EU
Multinational companies and their trade associations
States
Political Parties
Government departments, Quangos, National NGOs
Regulators
Courts
Local government
Local councils, trade boards, planning executives,
Parish councils, Community Groups, local trade associations
Neighbourhood watch
THE BOTTOM

Firstly, up. There is always someone above you in the great pyramid of societal organisation. The compromiser can easily blame their lack of helpfulness on the constraints placed on them by any of the bodies above them. They may claim that they can't move without their agreement. Those above have the real power, so take it up with them. Simultaneously, the excuser can look down, pretending to care about the opinions of those they have power over. In a spirit of democracy they may wish to devolve the decision as far away from them as possible. It's better to take the decision closer to the 'ground', meaning you waste time consultation and referring, surveying and sampling, when the compromiser who has the power will make up his own mind anyway. Trying to get the right people interested and motivated can take years. Why is this the case?

Nobody feels responsible...

The multiple layers of hierarchy in our globally connected world do strange things to our sense of duty and responsibility. There is a tension between an extended sense of connection with the ills of the world, brought home to us by the use of forced labour in the chocolate bar we enjoy, and the subtle, pervading sense of power-lessness which comes with being a small fish in a massive global pond. Apathy and helplessness are strange bedfellows with a sense of global citizenship.

I'm at a loss to explain my own inconsistencies of behaviour on this point, let alone those of wider society. We console ourselves, feeling we care about something, conceiving of ourselves as being not all that bad compared to some people who just flat don't care. But we never translate that 'care' into any specific action.

The immediate task before us is shifting someone, *anyone*, from their position of it "not being our problem". Campaigners on development issues stated this succinctly when tackling the developing country debt crisis. Many are confronted with global scale problems which they, as a mid-level manager in the IMF, or a very junior minister in cabinet, can feel powerless to assist, and that it is simply not worth their effort to care. Writing in 1988 - before the movement for voluntary debt relief had taken off – the political scientist Susan George wrote that where global crises are not the 'international civil servants' concern', "we must try to make it *someone's* concern".[68]

A successful campaign involving a noticeable public angle is one way to 'get someone to care'. Staying with the debt relief issue as our context, the work of Jubilee 2000, an umbrella group of NGOs and other bodies deserves special mention. Using inspiration from Christian history and theology for the idea of a 'jubilee' year - a cancellation of debt - in 1998 they organised the forming of a human chain around the venue for a meeting of the G7. In the words of Anthony Payne, professor of politics at the university of Sheffield:

"The effect was to transform the HIPC initiative from being a highly technical matter of concern in the main only to the IMF, the World Bank and their immediate clients and critics to a major political issue that demanded the attention of all the leaders of the G7 states."[69]

Of course, growing concern about an issue doesn't transfer automatically into changed behaviour. Awareness of climate change has grown massively in the last decade, yet our flying, driving and domestic energy use has risen steadily. Being concerned about something enough to tell a pollster that you are concerned does not mean that you really understand the issue, its drivers or its causes, or that you intend to do anything about it. More information does not necessarily solve this problem as we have seen, since we may become so realistic as to be hopeless. Allayed to our lack of responsibility is a sense of inadequacy.

Why is it so hard to get someone to move from a state of caring about something but doing nothing, into a state where their cares *and* behaviours are consistent? Some suggest that regretting something may be a powerful motivator. In many public discourses, we preach the 'regrets' that will come if we don't act right now, conjuring up future scenarios which could be avoided as we discussed in the first chapter.

But regrets do not apply equally to all kinds of action. We need to recognise the role that emotions play in our decision making, especially that which is sub-conscious. Feelings of regret are powerful, but they attach more to specific actions than inaction. We will feel more regret if we actually do something than if we just fail to do it. Research has demonstrated this phenomena this in relation to changing our answers on examinations.[70] Teachers may tell us to trust our instincts and not to change our first answer. But the evidence suggests the exact opposite - that the majority of answers changed are from wrong to right, and that most people who change their answers improve their scores. If that is the case, then why do we not change our answers more? Simply, there is much more at stake emotionally if you decided to change a right answer to a wrong one. You will feel that you cheated yourself much more deeply than if you suspected you might have the answer wrong, but did nothing. After all, it was only a hunch. If you had actually changed your answer, you had physically put the right one down and then removed it, and but for your stupid decision you would have done better. We are more comfortable with the consequences failing to act than the act of failing.

Something like this will express itself when people or organisations are asked to back a campaign or idea. You clearly have more to lose if you nail your colours to the mast decisively than if you just ignore it. It would be more regretful to back a loser than fail to be associated with an eventual winner, and you may have more to lose by failing than by winning. And so we find another excuse for our inaction.

...And Everybody Feels Powerless

Once someone has been persuaded to care about something, the next step is just as tricky. How do they make changes in their personal or professional life to reflect their new found concerns, and how do they influence the organisations of which they are part to start considering the issue? Apathy has been reversed, but how do they actually begin to deal with the problems? We only have so much resource, so much spare time and mental capacity, without taking on saving the world as well. It surely must be someone else's problem.

Some will consider themselves to be "the wrong person" out of an undue sense of deference to authority. This attitude was prevalent in early Victorian society, and lasted into the 20th Century in varying degrees, with a clear sense of class boundaries and "knowing one's place". Trust in one's political leaders was much more commonplace in an age before mass media. This is not to suggest that there never were political scandals, but before suffrage was universal, there was a much more rigid class system which supported a general respect and obedience to authority. The attitude was observable in all levels of society. There is usually someone above you, in authority. Few people worked for themselves, or in more egalitarian environments. At least the workplace has changed. Many industries have done away with traditional hierarchies, moving managers out of private offices and onto open-plan work-spaces.

However, this 'authority' has been abused. In the UK, respect for our political masters is at a very low ebb, following decades of spin, sleaze, and the crowning glory of the expenses scandal. Erosion of trust in those who are supposed to run things leaves us in a quandary, since we can no longer leave the management of important things to them and assume that they will be dealt with, but we feel powerless to suggest solutions. A growing sense of dis-trust in various controlling systems in the world economy has given birth to the 'Occupy' movements, for example. The power lies with us, since we delegated it to those democratically elected representatives who abused it, or so goes the argument. But how do you reform the entire financial system? We swing endlessly from apathy to powerlessness, and back again. Sooner or later we stop caring, get comfortable and compromise.

Understanding Apathy

It can be true that something is just not your problem. At university my room telephone number was one digit different from the library collections desk. People would often call me convinced they had the right number, and insist that I deal with the inquiry. My protestations were valid. I truthfully wasn't the right person.[71] Excluding the entirely plausible scenario of it genuinely not being our job, failing to do something about a problem which we could ameliorate is rooted in apathy.

At a national level, some apathy is not necessarily a bad thing. The fact that some people simply do not care about political life in a given country is in fact pretty useful. Before you start thinking that I am advocating the kind of one party rule observed in autocracies, hear me out. In the 1950's, theories began to emerge regarding this very idea - that a functional democracy would be impossible were every citizen to engage deeply and passionately on every issue. Conversely, some apathy is not born of carelessness or a failure to regard as important those issues which should be meaningful to the citizen, but of contentment. If I have no great struggles, if I have no great concerns, if my life is generally pretty good, then I have no real stake in the political process. This is one aspect of apathy - the active exercise of free will, the choice not to involve oneself in public life. If the individual has little to gain from participating, then rational self-interest will win out. Similarly, if they face manifest injustice, they have much more to gain from participation, exceeding the opportunity cost of doing so. You may also have a very well informed and critically weighed set of beliefs and values, which you simply do not believe worth sharing. In all of these *examples*, apathy is the public face of an actual, rational decision not to care.

The second aspect is altogether more troubling, and applies more to organisations, departments or other agencies. This is a more situational state of apathy, not a choice you decide on based on your own lack of dis-satisfaction, but something imposed on you from above, handed down and inferred by a general feeling of powerlessness, ignorance and perhaps even malevolent manipulation by those in power above you. Leaders of organisations can feel like a very small drop in a very large and choppy ocean. This 'situational apathy' is not an all consuming state of mind, applying to all elements of our collective psyche. Rather, it will be expressed towards particular issues. An organisation may care deeply about environmental issues, but be apathetic as regards human rights. A paradoxical attitude similar to this often surfaces among animal rights campaigners, the most extreme of whom consider it acceptable to abuse human life in the name of protecting animal life, meeting cruelty with greater cruelty. There is an apathy about human rights in such arguments, leading itself into an incongruity which demonstrates the complexity of dealing with apathetic attitudes and opposition.

Is non-participation in an issue a genuine expression of choice and hence an excuse, or is it a non-decision? In the political field, the latter may be more common. Participation in elections is linked to levels of education and earnings. Your non-participation may not be a glorious expression of your free choice not to care, but a reflection of your inability to care in the first place. Even if you have all the facts, you may not possess the intellectual capacity to weigh them and make the decision. Certainly this problem is becoming more common in an age of constant drip feeds of information and short burst entertainment, culminating in what the German sociologist Marcuse calls "the atrophy of the mental organs for grasping the contradictions and the alternatives".[72] Finally, your life may be a struggle. You may work two jobs and be trying to raise a few children on your own. The world of politics seems strange and detached from your reality, and hence your lack of participation in the political process is not a 'choice' but a result of your circumstances. In the words of Mills (another social scientist), you may be "gripped by personal troubles but unaware of their true meaning and source".[73]

Where there is an active decision not to care, your tactics will be different to that where there has been no decision. In the first instance, we can assume some level of understanding of the issues. Perhaps you could move the person into appreciating what he or she would have to gain from adopting a particular cause or attitude. In any case your engagement will be substantive, regarding the issue, trying to create moral or economic pressure, highlighting the benefits and helping them avoid the costs. In the latter, your efforts will likely be situational. You may have to do all sorts of things behind the scenes to move someone from a state of situational apathy into a place where they can begin to discuss the issues with you.

The normative element is the tricky thing to deal with. It is easy to come up with a theory about why someone doesn't care about your cause and refuses to engage in the issue. But presumably you are reading this chapter because you feel that someone *should* care, and *should* do something about it. It would be a mistake to call all non-participation apathy, as we have seen above, but where people have free choice to begin to choose being non-apathetic, you can begin to 'nudge' them along in their understanding. Even labelling them as apathetic may rouse them from their slumber. In this scenario, the agent has the freedom to overcome their own apathy, and your role is one of empowerment.[74] In the second, they are not able to assess what should be important to them. All the fancy arguments and choice language in the world will have little effect, since they have no internal capacity or agency to awaken. The works must begin at an earlier stage.

Projection of Apathy

In an institutional context, leaders and those in power can project their mental state onto the entire organisation. Leaders dictate a group's appetite for risk, since no-one wants to rock the boat by suggesting lots of projects that they know will be met with scepticism, with every new idea being damped down. In such contexts, people with ideas just stop suggesting them. People begin to conform to the images projected onto them, and begin to project them internally. If a leader generally has a low appetite for risk or for new ideas, he can consider not just his role but that of his department to be set in stone, and hence will never take on new responsibilities.

In the nursing profession, psychological studies and investigations have revealed some interesting facets regarding this projection of apathy (Menzies Lyth, 1989). Specifically, in the nursing profession there was a discernible lack of faith in development through training. Many believed that nurses were 'born, not made' and that all nursing training should really consist of is to find people with 'the gift', or 'the calling' to be a nurse, and then provide them with the tools, practical skills and the necessary practice at refining those skills. In a demanding and busy job, one laden with internal conflicts regarding personal responsi- bility for pain, discomfort and death which surrounds you every minute of every shift, entire groups set up defence mechanisms which help to deal with the tensions. Training and self-devel- opment appeared to be unnecessary, distractions from the 'real' work.

Imagine your idea is based on a belief or an observation that the skills of an average nurse could be improved with a regular investment in personal maturation as well as skills training. You would do well to be aware that the profession carries the defence mechanisms we talk about. Let's say that nurses have begun to de-personify their patients, referring to them as numbers and conditions rather than people. This is a logical defence mechanism designed to isolate the nurse from the suffering and pain, but it has consequences for the standard of care. The nurse begins to see someone as a catalogue of symptoms, not a person with emotional needs. Often emotional wholeness can be the road to recovery, or at least amelioration of symptoms. You suggest to the nursing fraternity that nurses be given some advanced training in active listening, or some very basic counselling (we're making all kinds of assumptions here, for the sake of simplicity. I know a great many in the nursing profession who have chosen to develop the 'bedside manner' which does so much to aide recovery).

And so to the argument against your proposal. Nurses aren't the right people. They have a vocation to care, to provide the basic physical care that patients in hospital need. They are stressed and tired. They do not need extra responsibilities. If you're that concerned about the mental and emotional welfare of patients, then employ some trained counsellors. But don't complicate the nurses' job any further. This seems to be a logical argument, but is in fact based on the assumption that training is next to useless. Nurses can't develop, so don't bother. In fact, developing nurses become distracted from their core tasks of monitoring, hygiene, administration of medicine etc.

Changing the profession might make this scenarios seem more familiar to you. Why train administrative staff in extra responsibilities? Why train manual labourers in administrative skills? If we are apathetic towards to notion that training is of value, we will consistently shun the opportunities to develop as an organisation and take on new challenges. Identifying this is important if you are engaging with a department or organisation which is happy to remain in its definable 'box'.

I'm just a cog in a wheel ...

Deference to those in authority is particularly interesting when embedded within an administrative hierarchy, or bureaucracy.[75] Authority is simple to understand where there is a general culture of submission to those above you in the hierarchy. If you feel powerless, you will take no initiative, and only act in accordance with the instructions given you from above. You are never the right person to do anything extra, unless so-and-so in the office tells you to. However, this is an oversimplification. As nice as it may sound, you would not really want to work for a department full of submissive followers of every decision, unable to solve even the most basic unexpected problem. We would want human ingenuity to be harnessed to some degree, and for others to recognise the problems that we cannot see.

Public officials are especially difficult to persuade, and are especially bound to rules and structures, accepting their place in the machine. Writing in 1957, Robert Merton classified the problems of various bureaucratic personalities, and explained the especially tricky position a public official finds himself in in relation to his clients.[76] :

> "They may be putting into practice political decisions with which they disagree; they are facing a public who cannot normally go elsewhere if their demands are unsatisfied, as they often can with private enterprise; and the justice of their acts is open to public scrutiny, by politicians and sometimes by courts of law. They are thus under particular pressure to ensure that their acts *are in conformity with rules.*"

Public officials also find themselves organised into more rigid career structures, with officials less likely to challenge the status quo if they feel their chances of promotion will be undermined. Conformity and lack of individualism can help a career in the civil service. Flashy entrepreneurs find gainful employment elsewhere. It is therefore a much tougher job to persuade a group of bureaucrats that they should something about a problem.

They are, however, well trained in carrying out instructions with skill and care. It's not always appropriate, but it's far easier to get a bureaucracy on side by going above them, and engaging their political or commercial masters on the issue. Bureaucrats and public officials have a subtle and under-appreciated role in applying policy. No matter how well defined a required action is given in the form of an instruction, bureaucrats are under particular stresses and pressures which lead them to interpret policy in ways different to those imagined. Hence they may not think of themselves as being the right people to engage regarding a problem, since they are just carrying out instruc-tions, but their interpretation is actually the problem you are trying to deal with.

I'm not suggesting that our bureaucrat consciously imposes his own values on a decision. In fact they, like anyone else, face pressures and uncertainties, and develop little habits to deal with them, making work life liveable. The social scientist Lipsky looked in detail at this phenomena in the early 1980s, and concluded that these habits 'effectively *become* the policies (that bureaucrats) carry out'.

If the way a decision is being carried out is the problem, then the solutions must be more creative. We must ask why people do not feel they are the right people to do something about an issue, or ask what pressures create the problematic attitudes, not just accept them as self-existence and try and change them without changing the context which created them in the first place. But when those services are public and free, such as social work, teaching or policing, demand is infinite. Our appetite for free things is not limited, and so the demands on a public servants time are similarly limitless - in theory, at least. Their resources will never match the problem, and they will always feel under pressure.[77]

Discretion

So far we have rather unfairly characterised bureaucrats and public officials as robotic followers of orders, slavish adherents to detailed policy with never a creative thought in their over worked and under-paid heads. No organisation can work without some delegation and hence some discretion in the managerial hierarchy. I may want something moved from one end of the warehouse to the other. As a time pressured manager, I do not want to be presented with a powerpoint of various options for moving the stuff for my consideration; I just want it moved. Further, people are less likely to stay in jobs where they are reduced to the status of robotic implementers of established procedure. There needs to be some element of creativity and imagination to make the job worth doing. The extent to which that person is 'watched' and their desire and willingness to break the rules are obviously other important factors. There may be established rules and ways of doing things, but if a new and better solution came along, most managers would be results orientated, and so endorse the new way, even though it was technically against the rules. It's therefore important to state that in any organisation, the rules are not static, the equivalent of the ten commandments given from a lofty higher power. They are functional expressions of convenience, and are fluid. Authority, as it relates to rules, is given to produce results. So if more convenient ways of getting results come about, the authority structures and the rules they enforce will change with them.

The word 'authority' may also be used slightly differently. Instead of having an authority bestowed *upon* you by external forces, you can *become* an authority on an issue yourself, or be assumed to be one by virtue of obtaining excellent personal and social skills. In every sphere of life, we depend on the received wisdom of others for delegated and assumed authority behind the opinions we hold. Authority to speak *to* a subject, and hence to pronounce on suggested changes in it or around it, can come with knowledge.

Authority to speak and make decisive contributions can therefore be acquired. If you do not feel like the right person to do something because you lack knowledge and insight, then become a person knowledgeable in that field. You can become a ten-minute expert in a subject with creative web-researching skills. You will not gain enough knowledge to out-manoeuvre a genuine expert, but you can acquire enough information to avoid making basic errors and not be sucked in by elementary deceptions and distractions.

The most difficult situation arises when your efforts at engaging with one group are referred to a higher authority which is simply not interested in your argument. The buck is passed to someone with more clout who won't use it. However, it may be that you have failed to understand a body's remit, and have couched the proposal in the wrong terms. If you are dealing with a watchdog body, they will not see it as their role to promote certain positive behaviours, but they will readily engage with complaints about negative behaviours. This should encourage us to think creatively about how we might profile an issue or push for a change. Here are some examples.

- If you can't get someone to agree to denounce something, can you get them to support the opposite case? So you might not be able to persuade someone that an activity is 'wrong', but you may get general support for a principle.

- If you can't get agreement on certain activities to be banned, aim for a statement of preferred best practice.

- If you can't get a behaviour to become mandatory, establish a rule on the 'comply or explain' basis. For example, you may have preferences for the best practice in the running of an organisation, but you can't get all parties to agree to the standards. So you establish the principle, and ask organisations to comply with it, or explain why they do not.

The department of time wasting

A final note of caution on the use of the excuse of the lack of responsibility by the comfortable compromiser; since beginning dialogue on an issue gives the illusion of progress, companies and government departments now staff whole teams of the wrong people for you to talk to - although you are never supposed to know that they are the wrong people. They take care to answer your questions, call you for regular updates and provide really excellent refreshments at their annual meetings. But as you suspect, they have very little actual power, do not make any decisions, are not involved in business strategy, and are in fact employed to put the best spin on a company's activities. This is a very cynical view of the modern Corporate Social

Responsibility manager and department. Of course there do exist some shining examples of such departments being integrated into business decision making, but they are few and far between. In meeting with those who have been employed to run 'interference', you will have good discussions which are ultimately fruitless. CSR Managers and HR Professionals are generally not that helpful if you want to engage properly with serious issues of business strategy, and you are better off pushing for representation from someone who has an actual, functional role within the business model of the company. Unfortunately, the right person to talk to you will be a very busy person, with little time on their hands.

And so we uncover yet another paradox. The wrong people will be more willing to talk than the right people. But uncovering the fact that you are talking to the 'wrong' people masquerading as the 'right' people is often difficult. Here, again, a healthy dose of cynicism is required. Perhaps the fact that someone *appears* willing to help should sound the alarm bells. If the first person you talked to was very conciliatory, then being nice to people like you might be part of their job description. Perhaps, then, the apathetic people are those with the real power, but are laden with worries and woe.

The key, then, is not to stop at the first obstacle you encounter, at the first person who claims to care but not to be responsible. If they care, then surely they know someone who is responsible, or at least may have a hunch? The comfortable compromiser is defined by his settled, happy state, his blissful inertia. Understanding their motivations, the psychological roots of apathy and their deference to real or perceived authority in their organisation will be helpful in moving them forward into actual decisions and actions about a topic. Something's wrong, and I have the power to do something useful to address it, and I now want to do it. Surely the comfortable compromiser - now much less comfortable than at the start - has no more excuses in his armoury?

Chapter 9

But It's Not The Right Time

Sadly, there is one more multi-purpose excuse which the comfortable compromiser can throw our way; even though we've failed in something similar, and things could be worse, we have made the necessary adjustments in order to do better this time and we're convinced we can do better. Even when we've agreed that what we're looking to do works well within the economic system, and we have the money to do it, and people seem generally in favour, and we have good evidence on our side. Even when we feel we can achieve change in spite of the systemic restrictions around us, and furthermore we feel that we really are the ones to do something about it. Once we've convinced the right people that they have the mandate and authority to make a changed, convinced them that said change is both in their interests financially and socially, mapped out the ways in which that change could be effected and learned from past mistakes, it may still all boil down to this excuse; it needs doing, but *not now*.

How do we move from good intentions to action, and what is attractive to us in timing a decision well? The timing of actions and the prioritising of equally competing goals is something we all deal with on a daily basis. Our time is finite, and our 'to-do' list, whether physical or mental, can seem to expand infinitely. The way in which we actually make decisions to do things can seem irrational. We choose to do easy things, putting off thinking about the harder things until later, delaying the inevitable, even though our procrastination wastes time and effort.

Breaking this down, we conceive of our decisions as being placed within an assumed time continuum. That is, it might not be the right time to do x because it is not currently affordable, but it is assumed by all parties that it might well be affordable in future. The timing argument makes the assumption that a decision could be made, and that there actually exists an optimum time for it to be made, but that now is not that time. Again, are such perfectly rational decisions ever attainable, or do we just do our best to make reasonably good decisions as and when we can?

Sometimes a decision to engage with an issue may expose internal divisions which those in power would much rather be keep hidden. Hence those in control of a political party may tell you it is not the right time to engage with, say, issues of sovereignty and our relationship with the EU around election time, since the issue is very divisive within the party and the public will be put off by in-fighting, leading to electoral losses. People seeking to control the agenda will try desperately to prevent an issue getting the oxygen of publicity. But they couldn't tell you that the issue would never be discussed, since it is clearly an important and difficult question. One option to put you off is to claim that now is the wrong time. They are comfortable in their compromise, and will use the timing argument as an excuse not to discuss this difficult issue.

In fact, there may well never be a 'right' time on our imaginary continuum to expose a divisive issue, because society as a whole has settled into a relatively easy pattern. We are in love with 'laissez-faire'. The term 'laissez faire' has been adopted to describe this general attitude to leave things well alone. DA Turner summarises our love of laissez faire in his book "Hope: the General Theory of Improvement, Setback and Forethought", referring to the market economics of Adam Smith and the necessity of letting rational self interest run its course:[78]

"It offers a very comforting doctrine for those whom it favours. It encourages the modern preference for not interfering; since tinkering with any delicate mechanism tempts catastrophe."

When it comes to changing things we don't really fully understand, we are reluctant; better not to rock the boat. But we all interfere with things, in small ways, all the time:

"...Yet every sales campaign, every take-over bid, every interest-rate hike seeks to do precisely that. Because interfering is what humans can never resist doing".

Our appetite for risk is obviously higher where there is more chance of a reward coming our way. We will interfere with things like interest rates and product sales since the benefits will come directly back to us. It's always the right time to better position yourself for the annual bonus, or to hit your weekly targets. When the benefit is an improvement to overall welfare, non-attributable to any one person, we are much more 'hands off', afraid of 'tinkering' with the machine.

In the latter half of the twentieth century and the start of the twenty first, political ideology has weakened. There are far fewer radical or ideological options. Whereas in the past politics was a clear divide between conservatives and liberals, capitalists and socialists, in Europe at least we see the majority of political parties occupying a centrist compromise position, assuming markets are the least worst way of organising our shared lives. The status quo does OK for most people, and seems to produce a sort of uneasy equilibrium. Politics, especially if you are in charge, then becomes a matter of letting no single issue get too prominent, and maintaining the status quo. Issues are managed, and there is never a right time to do anything.

The shifting paradigm
This illustrates that the structure of society and its prevailing beliefs

sometimes need to shift before change is possible. We see this most often when looking back into history and seeing some line of reasoning which appears manifestly abhorrent to modern understanding. In the case of slavery, over and above the arguments of necessity and value were arguments of racial supremacy.

Society at that time still carried echoes of feudal hierarchy. Class struggle had yet to be fully appreciated. Instead, class systems dominated societies, with social mobility an emerging phenomena. In a speech given in 1858, James Henry Hammond voiced a common argument - that slavery was a normal and essential part of the very structure of society:

> "In all social systems there must be a class to do the menial duties, to perform the drudgery of life. That is, a class requiring but a low order of intellect and but little skill. . . Such a class you must have, or you would not have that other class which leads progress, civilisation and refinement. It constitutes the very mud-sill (foundation) of society and of political government. ... Fortunately for the South, she found a race adapted to that purpose to her hand. A race inferior to her own, but eminently qualified in temper, in vigour, in capacity to stand the climate, to answer all her purposes. We use them for our purpose, and call them slaves."[79]

Viewed from a 21st century perspective, such arguments seem repugnant. Much has changed in global society since, as ideas of individual liberty, socialism and multiculturalism have taken hold.[80] As paternalism crumbled and traditional elites toppled in a wave of democratic awareness, slavery was defeated. In many cases, an idea or a campaign must wait until the right time, until society is willing and able to address an issue - but this did not stop the abolitionists campaigning on the issue, winning over hearts and minds until the attitudes in society reached a tipping point.

Crisis moments

Just when the opportunity seems least likely to appear, a crisis can arise which reopens the whole debate, and often redefines it, doing the paradigm shifting work which is necessary. Crises do not always transform into changes in public opinion, but public disasters can become moments of 'public epiphany'. The debate around an issue can change overnight from one of slow, glacier-like progress to rapid response, all due to the external stimuli of a crisis.

The debate over the use of nuclear power and the effect of crisis moments is intriguing, and in particular the debate in Germany over the continued use of nuclear power for domestic energy production. In late 2010, the debate was all but settled. Germany has a long history of investment in nuclear power, its utilities leading Europe in expertise in the technology. In 2011 it had seventeen operating reactors, and had only just reversed a decision to phase out their use by 2022, opting to continue their operation to help 'keep the lights on'. Nuclear reactors were no small beer in Germany, providing nearly one quarter of this developed industrial nation's energy needs, practically carbon free.

The green lobby has had a great deal of traction in liberal leaning Germany given the Green party's position as king maker in a proportionally elected democracy, as evidenced by the attractive subsidy regime afforded to small-scale solar power despite Germany possessing a relatively inferior solar resource. By and large, the green lobby's concerns on nuclear power - safety, costs and environmental legacy - had been met and defeated with arguments of necessity. Yes, its ageing fleet of reactors had issues. But the reality of increasing energy demand and the need to promote bridging technologies to the low carbon economy tie the hands of government. Extending the life of its nuclear plants was a difficult choice, but one which made economic sense for the country. After all, nuclear power in developed countries has a good safety record. The Chernobyl incident casts a shadow over the industry, but no reactor of such a poor design has been built in a democratic country for civil use. Compared with just about every other form of power, it is safe, clean, reliable and delivers power in sufficient magnitudes to feed a modern industrial nation such as Germany. The greens were up against a very comfortable compromise. There might be issues, but given our need for energy, is now the right time to tinker with our energy generation system?

Then in 2011 one event changed everything. The Fukushima nuclear incident was a crisis in the industry, an opportunity for the green lobby and a disaster for those defending the technology.

The initial stories of devastation quickly gave way to one of apocalyptic pseudo-melodrama. A nuclear power plant had been engulfed by a tsunami and had lost power to its cooling pumps. It was dangerously overheating, and explosions were being reported. Nuclear meltdown and another Chernobyl were on our hands. Fear ran riot in developed economies which had recently re-committed to a new breed of nuclear power. The media gleefully fed this fear. British authorities requested a safety review of its planned new reactors based on lesson learned after the Fukushima incident thankfully subsided. It seemed to be forgotten at this point that 24,000 people had been killed by the waves, and that no-one had yet died at Fukushima due to the nuclear meltdown. [81]

In Germany, the response was swift and decisive. Public fears over nuclear power were fuelled by the constant drip feed of fear from the 24-hour news coverage of Fukushima. Nuclear power is poorly understood in wider society, and fanciful claims were made regarding the dangers and risks. To be sure, the incident was incredibly serious. But claims of the risk of a nuclear explosion akin to that seen in Hiroshima were incorrect to anyone with an understanding of nuclear physics.[82] Claims of 'contaminated' water supplies and food stuffs were made, without any understanding of the dosage needed to be fatal, or even the very different characteristics of the different types of radiation. The turnaround was abrupt - Germany cancelled its investment in nuclear power and announced the closure of seven nuclear power stations. Nuclear power was dangerous - anyone watching the TV could see that.[83]

Except - how dangerous, exactly? Compared to what? Had anyone actually died at the plant yet, due to the issues with the reactor as opposed to the tsunami? Had it reached meltdown, or had it been largely controlled? When power was lost, the control rods automatically inserted into the reactor, stopping the reaction dead. The heating came from the used fuel, not the continued reaction. This is a design feature of advanced reactors which make it utterly different from the Chernobyl reactor. In just about the worst case scenario for a nuclear power plant, the system of containment had worked well, disaster response had been efficient and the worst impact had come from the loss of power to the Japanese grid. The long term impacts are yet to be understood or realised - but in terms of great industrial disasters, this ranks pretty far down the list in terms of immediate harm. The worst nuclear incident for two decades; but compared to the alternatives, how serious was it?

To take things further, how well did the Fukushima example translate to the specific risks posed by the German use of nuclear power? Not very well, in fact. Well designed nuclear reactors are safe - just don't build them near earthquake zones. The Fukushima disaster came not through a catastrophic system failure, but a failure to adequately manage risk. The risk to the plant in the event of a tsunami had been assessed, and a retaining wall built at a height thought adequate to protect the plant from a wave of historically high dimensions. In reality, the plans were proved inadequate by a once-in-a-lifetime wave which overwhelmed the cooling pumps. Germany faces no such risks. It is in a seismically stable area. It only has one shoreline. How did the Fukushima disaster mean *anything* to the German nuclear industry, which has very different risks, adequately managed in design features? And what of the alternatives? What of the thousands who lose their lives in the coal mining industry each year, or the oil riggers who daily risk injury and death in deepwater drilling operations? Nuclear power definitely carries risks - but compared to other viable sources of power and the full impact of their supply chains its overall safety record stacks up well. Never underestimate the power of a misunderstood crisis.

Our old friend the cognitive bias rears its ambiguously appreciated head once more when we consider timing, and the effect of more recent events on our perception of relative probability and risk. Put simply, more recent events, or events which were particularly vivid or shocking will not just live longer in the public memory, but will be subliminally attributed with more causal 'weight' than they deserve. As we will see in detail below, people in the world currently consider nuclear power to be much more risky than it in fact is due to the prevalence in the media this year of the worst nuclear incident since the last one. It is not a coincidence that the a preference for nuclear power was emerging after a protracted period of relative safety. Now that Fukushima is firmly lodged in our collective minds, and the crisis made more vivid by the kind of 24-hour news coverage which did not exist during the Chernobyl incident, there is a generally feeling the nuclear power is far more dangerous than it actually is. The public crisis affects our collective ability to make a genuinely rational decision, for better or worse. Such a shock can present something in a more favourable or worse light, and the opposing sides on a debate will be quick to exploit it.

Timing and the nature of the problem

Some issues of timing don't relate to the likelihood of success, but the necessity of it. Some social problems such as slavery and lack of female suffrage were problems which came of age in terms of public will to tackle them, but the problem was a continuing one. It this sense the timing didn't really matter - there just had to be enough of an appetite to get stuck in to a very difficult issue, reflecting the underlying shifting paradigm. In these kinds of policy situations, we need men and women of conviction, courage and persistence, since there will be no 'right' time to deal with the issue.

However, some problems have specific windows of opportunity which are more technically defined, especially in the environmental debate, meaning that the generalised timing excuse has much less authority. The right time to do something about climate change is now, while there is a chance of our actions having any effect. The right time to object to the effect of a new building obscuring your view is not when it has been built, but before, during the planning process. Our approach in these situations will necessarily be different, since we will have to force people *not* to do things they really want to do. The nature of the problem defines the right time to do something about it. If the window of opportunity is narrow, then the short timing can be used to create pressure on the decision makers above you.

That is not to suggest that a problem should be ignored just because the best time to have done something about them has passed. If your next door neighbour built that unsightly gazebo which blocks all the light of your garden without planning permission, then the fact that it has already been built means little. The person acting without the required authority took the risk that his actions would be challenged and decided to take it, so he bears the risk of financial penalty for removing the illegal gazebo. Companies often use this approach, presenting an action as 'fait accompli' in the hope that regulators and other enforcement officials will be too tired to prosecute, or susceptible to bribes to make the whole problem disappear. A natural resources company once took this approach, building an aluminium smelter before it had gained permission for the bauxite mine needed to power it, in the hope that the a relatively pro-business regulator would look at the fact that the company had already committed large sums to the building of the smelter and approve it on the basis that the time to reject the mine had passed since the smelter had already been built. If there was a fine to be paid, they would pay it; it would be small in comparison to the income from 30 years of successful mining and smelting in the area.[84]

If you gamble by creating facts on the ground before the relevant permissions have been attained, you bear the risk of having to act retrospectively to rectify them. Similar situations arise when occupying forces begin to construct dwellings and civilian infrastructure on occupied land. These attempts to create 'facts on the ground' are an effort to legitimise and realise claims to the land itself. The timing argument is linked to that of efficiency, as they assume that many will back the actions already taken rather than force the occupying power to remove the infrastructure, wasting the resources committed. The bigger the investments and the cosier the relationship with those in authority, the more likely that such actions will succeed.

How do we identify the 'right time', especially given all we have said about the 'windows of opportunity' afforded by circumstances? Clearly we would all like to take risks when we are most likely to succeed. As with every argument, in and of itself it may be valid, but it often acts as the final manifestation of the other arguments. Now may not be the right time to buy that car because we're still paying off our credit cards. It may not be the right time to hire that additional staff member since the employment tribunal has yet to rule on the discrimination case. Both these arguments are in fact ones of affordability and budget.

We must make a distinction between timing in terms of financial viability, which we've dealt with in much more detail in a previous chapter, and that of the likelihood of success.

Choosing the right moment can depend on many factors. Firstly, there is political will. Your organisation will likely sit on one end or other of the political spectrum. The kind of changes you would like to make will be more likely to be effected if the current government is sympathetic to your aims. Secondly, it may depend on popular will and opinion. Crises as discussed above work in this space, turning small issues into career-defining problems. If you are able to track public opinion on general matters, you may well identify more appropriate times to push for change. Thirdly, economic scenarios. We are constant in our continuing transition in and out of recession. It's the wrong time because we're just coming out of a recession, and we're only just finding our feet, the economy has only just recovered, we can't do anything major to disrupt things now. Or we're just going *into* a recession, we need to prepare for austerity, batten down the hatches and make serious decisions. I have frequently heard both arguments pronounced simultaneously.

Decisions and Emotions

When you fear the timing excuse, its use will come from that person's emotions and state of mind. Emotions, and particularly the feeling of self-esteem, are the wildcard which can make all our logical strategising come to nought.[85] We may have built a water tight economic, socially and environmentally optional case, got everyone onside, and got all the funding, but the decision can still go against us if the maker of that decision doesn't 'feel' it's the right time, at some gut emotional level.

You'll likely never know that emotion is playing the key role. Our true feelings may be hidden behind any of the standard objections which we've explored so far. In our increasingly touchy-feely world, we are increasingly using emotional language to justify our choices. Regardless of the dangers of following our emotions in the moment, trumping our usually observed wisdom, we have begun to identify ourselves more and more and emotional creatures we explain our actions in terms of our emotions. Some modes of thought have seen emotion as clouding rationality, certainly in late Victorian stereotypes of the hysterical 'emotional' woman, compared with the cool, rational man. But emotion plays an important role in decision making, because we are social beings.

If plan making is about gathering information, deciding on a method for dealing with a problem and then executing it, we can see how emotion might have interesting effects on the process. If we are fearful, we may focus more time and effort on identifying threats to our existence. If we are care-free and happy, we may underestimate threats. Our emotional state may also directly affect how we remember our past, emphasising our failures or successes in equal measure, perhaps wrongfully attributing greater importance to a few factors. Fear may lead us to prefer running away from the problem entirely rather than staying to deal with it. If a decision is associated with positive emotions, we may act to ensure that we feel that way again, repeating our actions. These are all useful traits, and probably necessary from an evolution point of view. It feels good to have our hunger satisfied, so we learn that eating is good. However, our positive emotions may be masking harm we are doing to ourself, so feeding our hunger become over-eating and gaining excessive weight. Emotions affect the way we make decisions in all kinds ways.

Shame and pride are the two emotions identified as having particular effects on self-esteem, and hence the decision making process (Fessler).[86] Imagine the story of young men getting involved in fatal violence developing from a dispute over a trivial amount of money, the difference of a few coins in the amount of a taxi fare. The elders of the village wonder openly at the 'madness' that led men to fight over such meagre sums - the rational cost-benefit analysis would never lead anyone to risk getting murdered over a marginal price disagreement, but the young men understand the overwhelming need to maintain one's pride. If there are norms of behaviour, in this example, the norm that you 'be a man' and stand up for yourself in front of women, then you experience negative emotion and social consequences if you fail to live up to that norm. Conversely, if you live up to the expected standards of behaviour, you feel more positively about yourself, as Fessler notes:

"It appears that when people feel either intense shame or intense anger, they disregard both the likelihood that a given goal will be achieved and the potential costs entailed if failure occurs, and instead choose a course of action solely designed to maximise benefits".[87]

Having feelings of low self-esteem tends to make you more conservative and less likely to take risks, whereas someone with strong sense of self-worth will seek new opportunities more readily, being more confident that they have talents which are in need of new outlets. However, this is generally true when decisions are made in advance. In the heat of the moment, low-self esteem may lead you into making much more rash decisions than you usually would. Our fear, hatred and self-loathing may lead us into making these rash, risky decisions which may see us lose everything, but they may also see us talk ourselves out of ever taking any risk.

Emotions affect the decision maker in three main ways. Firstly, they exist in the background, not specifically related to the task or decision in hand, but influencing it. If I have had a very stressful week at work, I may play football in a particularly aggressive manner, manifesting anger towards the other players which they did not elicit, making that tackle which I knew I shouldn't. I may have had an argument with someone, and wish to create more problems for them, so I do a task in a particular way, expressing revenge. These background emotions can also cause is to just to choose less-than-best outcomes, but can affect the decision making process.

Second, there are emotions arising from the task itself - be it stress, tension, anxiety, joy or exhilaration. When faced with more difficult and more complex choices, we may slip away from more cold calculations and tend to pay more importance to those with strong positive or negative emotions attached to them. Such task-related emotions may lead us into behaviours which don't help - panic, excessive attention to another's action and plain avoidance of the task itself.

Thirdly, our emotions may relate to the anticipated outcome. If we can imagine that a set of negative emotions may attach themselves to a particular course of action, we will rather obviously be less likely to choose it. Anticipated regret can stop us risking new things, just as anticipated joy can lead us to take the same risk. For our purposes, these last two would seem to be the most important. If we anticipate increased stress or losing opportunities for happiness, we will oppose a decision, even if it may potentially lead to a socially optimum outcome.

Emotions do not just affect us individually, They show themselves differently according to our social context. I can watch a funny film on my own, and never once laugh out loud, whereas watching the same film with friends or in the cinema will produce very different and louder responses to the same jokes.

Timing and risk

All changes involve an element of risk, a metaphorical rolling of the dice. You might be on a three, but the fear of ending up with a one rules out your ever risking it all for a 5 or a 6. There is never a 'perfect' time to do anything. Whether it be a personal decision such as getting married, or buying a house, there will always be some niggling doubt that you should put things off for just a little bit longer. The marriage example is a good one. I'm reliably informed by those with long and stable partnerships that nothing really prepares you for being married quite like being married, so once you and your significant other have decided that marriage is for you, then you should just bite the bullet and get on with it. Once certain decisions have been made, they provide enough solidity on which to base the rest of the uncertainty. I might not know what lies ahead, but I know the other person, and my trust in them makes it all OK. I might not know how my new business will survive its first year, but we have decided on a product and we're going to have a shot.

The pivoting principle here is 'enough' - reaching a threshold of confidence in your argument or plan so that you will 'roll the dice'. Is there *enough* proof of the benefits, *enough* proof of the existence of the opportunity? In models of decision making, we like to think we make the best choice based on full disclosure of all the facts and full knowledge of all the effects of our actions. Real life does not afford us this luxury, so we seek to make a pretty good decision based on the best information we have available to us at the time, often aware of the very things we 'don't know'.[88]

Satisficing - the route to happiness

The word 'satisficing' was coined by Herbert Simon in the 1950's combining the words 'suffice' and 'satisfy'. As a concept, it has much to recommend itself to those trying to cajole the comfortable compromiser into action. As we have seen in the last chapter, and infer from our previous exploration of the way in which we make decisions, there really is no one perfect time to do anything. If we wait for it, we will wait for ever.

It is therefore better not to wait until all the variables suggest that the action will be successful if executed now, but to identify a few fundamental indicators which will give our action a high change of success. At the core of this approach to life is our conception of the results of our actions - are we looking to maximise every decision we make, or are we happy to 'satisfice', i.e.make a pretty good decision and be happy with it, and not waste time thinking up fictional scenarios in which we may have got the decisions just a few percent better.

A 'satisficer' typically has a better life than a 'maximiser'. Even if they occasionally miss out on making spectacular gains through excellent decisions, they have enough spare energy in which to enjoy the fruits of their pretty good decisions. The timing excuse can be the last resort of a perfectionist, one who is reluctant to commit to taking action for fear that waiting a little longer will increase the likelihood of success by some small increment. If has echoes of the fear of failure discussed in chapter two. The world in which we live faces many challenges, ones which need to move to address now, even if we don't have absolutely the most wonderful solution immediately at our fingertips. Now may not be the right time to maximise, but it can be the right time to 'satisfice'. The comfortable compromiser wants you to think that you have to wait until it's absolutely the *best* time to do something. That time may never come.

'Satisficing' is emphatically not an attitude of compromise. It still has a sense of purpose, and still makes a net contribution. It just accepts the constraints around it, and makes the best inter-vention it can. 'Satisficing' is in fact an antidote to compromise - it gives a person with the ability to weigh the issues a way to make decisions and take actions in seemingly intractable situa-tions. Encouraging a compromiser to think more like 'satisficer' will have many benefits, since it will help address every one of the common excuses which we have discussed.

Chapter 10

Epilogue

It is worth stressing this important point; clearly, there are certain ideas which are just plain dumb, just as there are perfectly valid excuses for inaction. I would like to raise just a few for each chapter:-

But It Could Be Worse. Yes, it really could be worse. Yes, that other colleague is annoying, but is it that bad?

But We've Tried Before - And Failed. Alchemy - getting gold from base metals - is impossible. Stop trying.

But We've Always Done It That Way - and that's because it's a very good way to do it. The umbrella is a very long-lived invention, a means for portable personal shelter from the rain. Forever, it seems, the working man or woman has prevented the ingress of precipitation by means of the umbrella. It works. It's cheap.

But The Economy Will Collapse - perhaps imposing a 100% tax rate on corporations might not be all that great an idea. Some economic policies are just plain dumb.

But We Can't Afford It - If I have £20 and want two DVD box sets which each cost £20 each, I can't have both. There can be effective limits to resources in micro-economic situations.

But 'The system' Won't Let Us - Rules and regulations may be set up to stop criminal activity which may be annoying to you.

Having to use all manner of security questions and passwords is annoying - why not simplify? But the people in charge of financial institutions have a duty to protect your money. The system won't let us bend - and for good reason, despite the inconvenience it causes.

But Our Statistics Said - If you take a survey and 90% of people are in favour, then it's probably OK to do something about it. Similarly, if the world's best minds sum up an opinion on an issue, it might just be worth trusting their conclusions based on their statistics.

But We're Not The Right People - We can't do everything, and not everything is your job. It's no use asking a plumber to help you plan your vegetable patch.

But It's Not The Right Time - There are windows of opportunity which are worth waiting for. Doing anything at sea in terrible weather is a bad idea - it really is much better to wait for the summer and calmer waters.

What now?

The comfortable compromiser has been a straw man which we have moulded for our purposes and knocked down, embodying all the worst personality traits you are likely to encounter, having an answer to everything you say and having tried everything you ever suggest. In the field conditions of the workplace or the public sphere, such pure-bred compromisers are rare. Rather, it is more likely that you will hear echoes of many different people you know and work with in the excuses. The basis of our compromiser's excuses are in fact reasonable, logical decisions - but taken out of context and used for purposes other than those originally intended.

Or it may be that you see yourself in the compromiser's

personality, and hear your own voice in his excuses. Hopefully, this book will help you to realise those excuses which you have made use of, and act as a stimulus to re-evaluate your positions on some issues.

References

Jim Powell. *How the West Abolished Slavery* Palgrave Macmillan 2008

James D. Torr. *Slavery: opposing viewpoints in world history,* Greenhaven Press2003

Michael Craton, James Walvin & David Wright. *Black Slaves and the British Empire.* Longman, 1976

Edward Behr. *Prohibition; Thirteen Years That Changed America.* 1st North American Edition, Arcade Publishing 1996

Arthur Schopenhauer. *The Art of Always Being Right* Gibson Square Books Ltd; 1st ed. Edition 2004

Richard Feldman. *Reason and Argument.* Pearson; 2nd edition 1998

Mark Thornton. *The Economics of Prohibition* University of Utah Press (1991)

Joseph T. Hallinan. *Why We Make Mistakes.* 2009 Broadway Books; Reprint edition 2010

Charles Handy. *The Age of Unreason,* Random House Business, 1995

Adrian Furnham. *Management and Myths; Challenging business fads, fallacies and fashions,* Palgrave MacMillan 2004

John Williamson. *Voluntary approaches to debt relief* Institute for International Economics,U.S.; Revised edition 1990

Susan George. *A Fate Worse Than Debt.* Grove Press 1988

Anthony Payne. *The global politics of Unequal Development* Palgrave Macmillan 2005

Jeffrey D. Sachs. *Developing Country Debt and the World Economy* University of Chicago Press 1989

Jeffrey D. Sachs. *Common Wealth - Economics for a crowded planet* Penguin; First Thus edition 2009

Jeswalde W. Salacuse. *Making Global Deals - What every executive should know about negotiating abroad* Times Books; Reprint edition 1992

Roy J Lewicki, David M. Saunders, Bruce Barry. *Negotiation.* McGraw-Hill Higher Education 5th Edition 2006

Tom L. Beauchamp, Norman E. Bowie *Ethical Theory and Business* Pearson, 7th Edition 2004

John M. Bruce, Clyde Wilcox. *The Changing politics of Gun Control* Rowman & Littlefield 1998

Herbert Asher. *Polling and the Public; What Every Citizen Should Know* CQ Press 6th Edition 2004

William J. Vizzard. *Shots in the Dark.* Rowman & Littlefield Publishers 2000

Patrick Major. *Behind the Berlin Wall* Oxford University Press, USA, 2010

Mary Fulbrook. *The People's State* Yale University Press 2005

Nicholas Jones. *Soundbites and Spin Doctors* Victor Gollancz 1996

Robert J. Spitzer. *The Politics of Gun Control* Paradigm Publishers; 5 edition 2011

Lance Price. *The Spin Doctor's Diary* Hodder & Stoughton 2005

Robert Rückel (ed.). *GDR Guide - Everyday Life in a Long Gone State in 22 Chapters* Ddr Museum Verlag 2009

Russell Jacoby. *The End of Utopia* Basic Books 1999

Tom DeLuca. *The Two faces Of Political Apathy* Temple University Press,U.S 1995

Liz Jeffery. *Understanding Agency - Social Welfare and Change* Policy Press 2011

Isabel Menzies Lyth. *The Dynamics of the Social - Selected Essays* Free Association Books 1989

E.D. Watt. *Authority* Palgrave Macmillan 1982

Miley W. Merkhoffer. *Decision Science and Social Risk Management* Springer; 1 edition 1987

Aaron Lynch. *The Thought Contagion* Basic Books; Pbk. Ed edition 1996

Christopher Ham & Michael Hill. *The Policy Process in the Modern Capitalist State* Prentice-Hall; 2nd edition 1993

David Anthony Turner. *Hope: the General Theory of Improvement, Setback and Forethought.* Premise Books; First Edition 2007

Gigerenzer & Selten, Editors. *Bounded Rationality - The Adaptive Toolbox.* MIT Press; New edition 1999

Robert Boyer & Daniel Drache, Editors. *States Against Markets; the limits of globalization* Routledge 2000

Elcock, Jordan & Midwinter. *Budgeting in Local Government; Managing the Margins.* Longman 1989

Harlod L Smith. *The British Women's Suffrage Campaign* Longman 2nd Edition 2009

Joyce Marlow (ed.). *Votes For Women - The virago book of suffragettes* Virago Press Ltd; First Edition 2000

Ha Joon Chang. *The 23 things they don't tell you about capitalism* Allen Lane; First Edition 4th Impression edition 2011

Abhijit Banerjee & Esther Duflo. *Poor Economics: A Radical Rethinking of the Way to Fight Global Poverty* PublicAffairs,U.S. (9 Jun 2011) 2011

Robert Muller. *Science and Technology for Future Presidents* Princeton University Press, 2010

Andrew Szasz. *Shopping our way to safety* University of Minnesota Press 2007

Herman Daly. *Beyond Growth* Beacon Press; New edition 1997

Endnotes

1. We also agreed on an arbiter of all that was neutral; pre-coalition and the travails suffered by the Liberal Democrats, we used the 'Clegg Neutrality Threshold' as the line where good and evil met in glorious, apathetic neutrality. How things change . . .
2. Merkhoffer pg 20 citing Slovic et al 1983
3. Feldman, pg 199
4. For more on this, see Chapter 7
5. To take an auto-biographical turn, my own experiments with home brew in my student days were either dismal failures or dangerously successful. On one occasion, we waited 6 weeks before discovering we had managed to kill the yeast, resulting in a grainy, starchy, vomit inducing mess. On another, having included more than the recommended amount of sugar, we produced gut-rot of such staggering strength that it got you drunk from the toes up, producing a three day hangover replete with nausea comparable to being locked in a room with James Blunt playing on loop.
6. Lewicki, Saunders & Barry pg 61
7. Lewicki
8. Fischer 1964
9. Although, it is not essential. You can be dragged into the argument, in areas way beyond your expertise, losing valuable time and resource. If you feel something is wrong - manifestly harmful, unfair or corruptive, it is somebody's job to keep banging on about it until someone listens. Just because you can't solve a problem on your own doesn't disqualify you from alerting others to the problem.
10. http://www.foreignpolicy.com/articles/2011/01/02/where _do_bad_ideas_come_from?page=full
11. Walt, in the foreignpolicy.com article above

12. Which illustrates another great truth - be careful what you give away, as people will be very reluctant to pay for it in future.

13. Some might also claim that the 'middle' ignore the voice of the youth just as effectively. Whatever segment of society you find yourself in, or whatever generation you feel you belong to, you feel like no-one is listening to you, and are in fact listening to someone else.

14. Sachs "Common Wealth" 2008 pg 395

15. Powell pp 115

16. It is also necessary to draw a distinction between failure in creative or responsive work, and failure in every day tasks. Failure to effectively deal with administration is not a calibration, just inability to concentrate or evidence of incompetence.

17. Furnham, "Failing in Business" pg 57 Management myths

18. "Rethinking rationality" cited in Gigerenzer and Selten, pg 7

19. This is also an example of effective feedback - the robot which focuses on the ball is receiving feedback about its position relative to it.

20. The rules need not be based on factual or scientifically correct observations to still be useful. They may rest on cultural values which are inaccurate but do not precluded their usefulness. For example, Gigerenzer and Selten cite the example of effective navigational techniques which were effective despite being based on the erroneously held belief that the sun moved round the earth. The cultural belief did not stop the rule of thumb working well.

21. For an excellent explanation of the relative risks of different terrorist threats and their likelihood based on the principles of physics, please see the redoubtable Dr Muller's excellent book, "Physics for Future Presidents". If you haven't time I'll summarise; 9/11, in its exact form cannot happen again. Pilots were up until 9/11 instructed to cooperate with

hijackers. Usually, they just wanted to be flown to Cuba, or some other location, where negotiations would take place. Nobody had foreseen the likelihood of planes being exploited in their guise of a self-delivering payload of explosive (aviation fuel). It wouldn't happen now, in the same way. Pilots would not give up controls. Air marshals sit on flights. And passengers would not stand by and let things happen. The world has changed. But we still can't take nail clippers in our hand luggage.

22. Payne & Betman in "Bounded Rationality".
23. Peter M Told in "Bounded Rationality" pg 56
24. Abdolkarim Sadriek et al in "Bounded Rationality" pg 87
25. Lewicki et al pg 147
26. George, pg 262
27. The Military strategy of General Melchet, BBC Comedy's fictional military commander!
28. Feel free to use this description the next time you are asked to compile a rota, or decide on the colour of the walls in the dining room.
29. For the sake of completeness it must be mentioned that this theory has been challenged and refined, most notably by Dror. The reality probably sits somewhere between the rational and the incremental approaches.
30. Crouch, Farrell: Breaking the Path of Institutional Development?
31. Cited in Crouch, Farrell: Breaking the Path of Institutional Development?
32. The old joke goes something like this. How many (Insert name of denomination or group here) does it take to change a light bulb? "CHANGE?"
33. Although our society and its stress on consumerism is constantly reinventing the wheel. A trip to a supermarket will expose you to the toiletries aisle, with row after row of toothpastes, which are 95% the same as each other. Men use

razors which are constantly reinvented with sub-optimal outcomes. Previous generations made use of reusable single blade safety razors which could be sharpened. A good razor would last you years, and the quality of shave was excellent. Now we have 5 bladed replaceable cartridge models which offer no substantive advantage from the older models, apart from a marginally better shave, but with the added cost of buying cartridges. The wheel has been very successfully and lucratively reinvented, a means of generating additional income, producing more waste.

34. Speech in the Exeter Hall, London 11 Feb 1907; cited in 51 Virago

35. Ted Wragg, the famous education professor and writer once suggested the opposite - that reinventing the wheel was actually important. Otherwise Olympic Cyclists would never have carbon fibre rims, and truck wheels would still be made of wood.

36. Sachs, Common Wealth pg 316

37. Handy, the Age of Unreason pg 21

38. That the plastic bag issue has been so aggressively pursued in itself smacks of irrationality. The biggest environmental issues facing us include, among others, climate change, over-population, deforestation, loss of biodiversity, and water scarcity. And we're worried about plastic bags . . .

39. Of course, attempts to price in environmental factors have generally been problematic. The EU ETS has set carbon prices so high as to present power producers with large windfalls; establishing the 'right' level for an environmental tax is notoriously difficult. In fact, the difficulty in setting prices artificially underlies the main reason why people like to trust the markets, since they perform the process of price determination automatically, at least in theory.

40. A plot line from an advert run by a debt consolidation company in the mid 2000's in the UK.

41. Any debt is only as valuable as its likelihood of repayment or enforcement. For the private provider of finance in a country like the UK, the governance and enforcement of private debts is strong, hence debts retain their value. On the global scale, the larger the debt in relation to the size of the economy on which it is based, then generally speaking the greater the likelihood that it will be repaid in full. Hence the value of the debt to the loan maker actually decreases.

42. Although it is not completely free to do so, since every decision they make alters the interactions of different parts of the economy, having an affect on interest rates and other vitally important economic indicators.

43. Quoted in Elcock et al pg 8

44. Estimates from the 1980's suggest around 80% of local authority expenditure was 'spoken' for or mandatory.

45. Bearing in mind that steady expenditure may well reflect a very steady political environment, or a steady level of demand for services.

46. http://www.socialfinance.org.uk/work/sibs/criminaljustice

47. Hapgood, Cited in Merkhoffer pg 178

48. Hapgood, *supra*

49. Handy "The Age of Unreason" pg 57

50. probably

51. http://www.hse.gov.uk/myth

52. The official motto of the State of New Hampshire is "Live free or die" - I have never known whether this is a command or a claim, but it doesn't resonate with me. My own motto would be something more along the lines of "Live free or write a strongly worded letter to a National newspaper".

53. http://www.economist.com/node/16646044

54. Salacuse 1991

55. Baumgartner and Jones

56. We might also have a bias towards information presented to us in a certain way. If we are used to spreadsheets, we may

attribute greater worth to data provided in this form than in a graph or a log sheet. We may have a favoured way of collecting information in the first place. Or we may have a prejudice against a form of collection, such as a survey. In which case it's probably a bit rich to write a section on cognitive bias based on your own cognitive bias against surveys . . .

57. Behr pg 148.
58. And best imagined in the dulcet tones of Martin Sheen portraying fictional President Josiah Bartlett, immortalised in an episode of political drama, The West Wing.
59. Monkton pg 23 quoting "I N Fisher" 1956
60. Selten 1999
61. http://www.bbc.co.uk/news/magazine-11798317
62. Fischoff et al 1980, cited in Merkhoffer pg 157
63. Although the dynamic is shifting; I am a relatively well off young man, but I have not had a landline for 10 years. I rely exclusively on my mobile phone for personal calls; the only landline I ring with any consistency is my parents. My sample size is small, but I would assume the same to be true for my peers.
64. Quoted in Jacoby, pg 83ji887
65. http://www.guardian.co.uk/commentisfree/2011/jun/13/dodgy-data-journalism-politics
66. Feldman, pg 192-193
67. And also question their understanding of the principle of causality, as we discussed earlier.
68. A Fate Worse than Debt, 1988 pg7
69. Payne, pg 149
70. Kruger, quoted by Hallinan,
71. Although I have to admit, when someone became fixated on my number and refused to believe that I wasn't the library collections desk, and had called me three times in 5 minutes at 9am on a Saturday morning, I assumed the identity of the

collections desk and told the person on the other end of the line that his books had been extended on loan for another week.

72. Quoted in DeLuca pg 153

73. Quoted in DeLuca, pg 143

74. Although, even when the root cause of their apathy was personal, they may be still beyond rescue. "A person may be responsible for devolving into a state of apathy, now congealed into such a formidable obstacle that we think that the person no longer has the resources to break free" DeLuca pg 193

75. Authority may be derived from rules or structures, but it may also stem from a person's personality and character-istics. It's an authority which rests on the 'charisma' of its holder. This charismatic authority is very tricky to deal with. It may be a visionary leader, manager, who inspires loyalty and slavish devotion from his subordinates. This kind of authority, when deferred to, will not be undermined by sound argument since the person exercises authority apart from logic.

76. Cited in Ham & Hill pg 136

77. In which case they will sometimes be open to friendly offers of help.

78. D A Turner "Hope" pg 25

79. quoted in pp 18 Slavery, opposing viewpoints in world history.

80. Although it must be said that by no means all abolitionists were in favour of racial equality.

81. At least five people have died at the Fukushima plant. Four of these can be attributed to the effect of the earthquake. The fifth was a relief worker who suffered a heart attack. There may yet be more deaths from radiation exposure, but these will take months or years to manifest.

82. Since you ask, I have such an elementary understanding,

Since you ask I have such an elementary understanding, as I grew up under the maternal instruction of a physics teacher. The key confusion comes in the forms of fuel used in nuclear weapons and nuclear power generation. One is highly enriched uranium 235, concentrated to 98% in order to create the conditions for a runaway chain reaction. The other uses 3-5% U-235, enough to create a controllable, lower scale chain reaction. A nuclear power plant can explode and cause damage, but it is physically impossible for it to cause damage on the scale of a nuclear bomb. Recommended reading - chapter 7 of "Physics for Future Presidents" by Professor A Muller.

83. Although things are clearly more complex than the constraints of space demand. The decision is partly economic, as many see nuclear power only getting more expensive with growing long-term liabilities. But even if this is the basis, the crisis created the opportunity to rethink the investment decision.

84. Thankfully, the regulator in question was swayed by popular opinion, and the company was forced to bear the economic consequences of its aggressive stance.

85. Daniel M.T. Fessler in "Bounded Rationality"

86. Daniel M.T. Fessler in "Bounded Rationality"

87. "Bounded Rationality" pg 197

88. Those factors classified so aptly by Donald Rumsfeld as 'known unknowns'.

**BUSINESS
BOOKS**

Business Books encapsulates the freshest thinkers and the most successful practitioners in the areas of marketing, management, economics, finance and accounting, sustainable and ethical business, heart business, people management, leadership, motivation, biographies, business recovery and development and personal/executive development.